English Grammar Basics:

The Ultimate Crash Course with over 50 Exercises, Quizzes, Discussion Questions, and Easy to Understand Grammar Rules

By Crystal Carothers

# Contents

# Preface

Thank you for purchasing and downloading this book. I've written this book with the English language learner in mind, or for those who speak English as a second language. However, even if English is your native language, you can still benefit from this book, especially if you are one who makes grammar mistakes often or you lack understanding for the basic grammar rules of the English language. Even native English speakers are guilty of making basic grammar errors, which are more prevalent than ever. From emails to blog posts, these errors can be found everywhere. Grammar errors in our writing can be embarrassing and lead others to think that we are uneducated. The truth is that others judge us by our writing, even if it's a post on Facebook. If you go through and complete these exercises, you will be able to much more easily spot grammar errors in your own writing and in the writing of others. This book starts from the beginning, giving you the foundation of basic grammar principles for the English language.

Depending on which device you are using to view this book, the format will vary. I've worked hard to try to make the format as readable as possible, but since this is an eBook, and a textbook, this is easier said than done. Newer kindles will have much better format and readability than older versions. If the format from your device is unsettling or difficult to read, feel free to email me and I can send you a copy of the pdf version. (crystal_carothers@yahoo.com)

*How to Use This Book*

Each chapter of this book focuses on a grammar topic and the specific rules. After each rule, there are exercises to practice that specific rule. I recommend writing down your answers. When you complete the exercises, check your answers in the answers section. After checking your answers, if you have all or most of the answers correctly, you can skip the additional exercises and move on to the next chapter. However, if, after checking your answers to the preliminary exercises, you have a lot of incorrect answers, I would recommend doing the additional exercises and the quiz at the end of each chapter. Make sure to check your answers to the additional exercises before taking the quiz. I also recommend starting with chapter one. Skipping chapter one (parts of speech) might make other chapters harder to understand. I hope that you gain a better understanding of basic grammar concepts through this book.

Let's begin!

# Chapter 1: Parts of Speech (The Basics)

This is a very brief and basic overview of the parts of speech. Let's go over some definitions.

1.  Subject: a word or phrase that always comes at the beginning of the sentence before the verb. This is the focus of the sentence, or what the sentence is about. (I, you, he, she, it, they, we, at the beginning of the sentence are all subjects.)

    Example 1: *I* am at home. *(Subject = I)*
    Example 2: *My father* loves pizza. (Subject = *My father*)
    Example 3: *The blue car* is nice. (Subject = *The blue car*)

2.  Verb: A verb (v) is usually an action word (eat, sleep, read) although it can also be a state (be). The verb always comes after the subject in a sentence.

    Example 1: I *am* happy. (verb = am)
    Example 2: My father *loves* pizza. (verb = loves)
    Example 3: We *believe* her. (verb = believe)

3.  Noun/noun phrase: A noun (n) is a person, place or thing. It can also be an abstract idea (happiness). A noun phrase (np) is a group of words that together function as a noun (a nice car, my computer).

    Example 1: *New York* is *a great city*. (noun = New York / noun phrase = a great city)
    Example 2: *Mr. Smith* is not here. (noun = Mr. Smith)
    Example 3: Where are *my pants*? (noun= pants / noun phrase = my pants)

4.  Adjective: An adjective (adj.) is a word that describes a noun. An adjective usually comes after the *'be'* verb (She *is nice*) or before a noun (the *red* car).

    Example 1: I am *happy*. (adj. = happy)
    Example 2: The computer is *expensive*. (adj. = expensive)
    Example 3: My *little* sister is *here*. (adj. = little, here)

5.  Complement: a complement is a word or phrase that completes the sentence. The complement can be an adjective, noun, or an adjective or noun phrase, but it always comes after the verb. You don't always need a complement since some sentences in English are made up of Subject and verb only (ex: She fell.)

    Example 1: New York is *a great city*. (complement = a great city; this is also a noun phrase)
    Example 2: My father loves *pizza*. (complement = pizza; also a noun)
    Example 3: I am *happy*. (complement = happy; also an adjective)

*Rule 1: In English, almost all sentences follow the following format: [Subject + Verb + (Complement)]*

The complement is in (parentheses) because we don't always need a complement to have a complete sentence. Notice this in the following examples.

| Subject | Verb | Complement |
|---|---|---|
| I | have | five children. |
| He | is giving | a speech. |
| Mrs. Smith | is going to be | here next week. |
| The movie | will end | soon. |
| You | didn't know. | |
| We | are | students. |
| The children | fell. | |

Note that the Subject can also be a noun or noun phrase, and the complement can be an adjective, adjective phrase, noun or noun phrase.

Exercise 1

Directions: Read the following sentences and put the parts of speech in the correct place on the table. Number 1 is done for you.

1. We are at the park.
2. Timothy is not here.
3. My mother likes chicken soup.
4. I need some medicine.
5. My older sister lives with me.
6. Christmas is my favorite holiday.
7. My cats aren't eating their food.
8. The big table is old and dirty.
9. Mr. Ricky doesn't eat breakfast.
10. My aunt smokes cigarettes.

| Number | Subject | Verb | Complement |
|---|---|---|---|
| 1 | We | are | at the park |
| 2 | | | |
| 3 | | | |
| 4 | | | |
| 5 | | | |
| 6 | | | |
| 7 | | | |

| 8 | | | |
|---|---|---|---|
| 9 | | | |
| 10 | | | |

- Check your answers in the answers section

Exercise 2

Directions: Using the same sentences in exercise one, identify all the nouns, adjectives, and noun phrases. Number 1 is done for you.

| Number | Noun | Noun Phrase | Adjective |
|---|---|---|---|
| 1 | We, park | X | X |
| 2 | | | |
| 3 | | | |
| 4 | | | |
| 5 | | | |
| 6 | | | |
| 7 | | | |
| 8 | | | |
| 9 | | | |
| 10 | | | |

## Answers to Exercises Chapter 1

### Answers to Exercise 1:

| Number | Subject | Verb | Complement |
|---|---|---|---|
| 1 | We | are | at the park |
| 2 | Timothy | is not | here |
| 3 | My mother | likes | chicken soup |
| 4 | I | need | some medicine |
| 5 | My older sister | lives | with me |
| 6 | Christmas | is | my favorite holiday |
| 7 | My cats | aren't eating | their food |
| 8 | The big table | is | old and dirty |
| 9 | Mr. Ricky | doesn't eat | breakfast |
| 10 | My aunt | smokes | cigarettes |

### Answers to Exercise 2:

| Number | Noun | Noun Phrase | Adjective |
|---|---|---|---|
| 1 | We, park | X | X |
| 2 | Timothy | | here |
| 3 | mother, soup | my mother, chicken soup | chicken (because it describes the soup) |
| 4 | I | some medicine | X |
| 5 | me , sister | My older sister | older |
| 6 | Christmas, holiday | my favorite holiday | favorite |
| 7 | cats, food | My cats, food | their |
| 8 | table | the big table | big, old, dirty |
| 9 | Mr. Ricky, breakfast | X | X |
| 10 | aunt, cigarettes | My aunt | X |

Now that you have a better understanding of the parts of speech, let's move onto Chapter 2. Note that this is the only chapter that does not have additional exercises and activities.

## Chapter 2: The Be Verb

Test Your Knowledge: Find the Mistakes (Check your answers in the chapter titled "Answers" section)

1. I from San Francisco.
2. Where you are from?
3. She is come to the party.
4. Everything is Ok?
5. His not here right now.

*Rule 1: The "be" verb functions differently than all other verbs in English. It must be changed into [am, is, are] depending on the Subject (I, you, he, she, it, they, we, etc.)*

| Subject | Be verb (present tense) |
|---------|-------------------------|
| I | am |
| You | are |
| He | is |
| She | is |
| It | is |
| They | are |
| We | are |

Exercise 1

Directions: Fill in the blank with the correct form of the *be* verb (am, is, are)

Example: My mother _____ at home.

Answer: My mother.....*is*....... at home.

1. They _____ happy.
2. She _____ on the phone.
3. My computer _____ broken.
4. I _____ sure.
5. Her name _____ Sarah.
6. My father and I _____ on vacation.
7. My friend Charlie _____ lost.
8. We _____ in the library.
9. My shoes _____ dirty.

10. My shoe _____ clean.


*Rule 2: To construct a negative with the "be" verb, use "not" after the verb (am, is, are)*

Examples:

- I am *not* at home.
- She is *not* at the park.
- They are *not* happy.


Exercise 2

Directions: Fill in the blank with the correct form of the negative "be" verb

Example: My computer _____ cheap.

Answer: My computer………*is not*………cheap.


1. My brothers _____ here.
2. The cat _____ sick.
3. Sarah and I _____ at the park anymore.
4. The store _____ crowded right now.
5. My sister _____ married.
6. I _____ a doctor.


*Rule 3: To make a Yes/No question with the "be" verb, use the format:*

[be + subject + complement]

Examples:

| Be Verb (Is/ Am/ Are) | Subject | Complement |
|---|---|---|
| Are | you | at home? |
| Is | Mr. Smith | sick today? |
| Am | I | late? |


Common Mistake: *I'm late?*

First of all, never use a contraction (I'm) in a question. This may be fine in spoken English if you are simply repeating what someone said to confirm what has been said. However, in written English, the questions with the 'be' verb need to be in the form of a question: *Am I late?* (the subject *I* must come after the verb *am*).

Exercise 3

Directions: Use the words to create a Yes/No question using the "be" verb.

Example: (happy/you)

Answer: *Are you happy?*

1. at home/ my brother
2. sick/ they
3. the computer/ expensive
4. hot today/ it
5. good/ the waves
6. I/ in trouble
7. late/ we
8. your friends/ nice

*Rule 4: To make an Information question (Who, What, Where, When, Why, etc.) with the "be" verb, use the following format.*

[Wh word + be verb + subject + complement]

Remember that the subject decides which form of the be verb (am, is, are)

Examples:

| Wh word | (is/ am/ are) | Subject | (complement) |
|---------|---------------|---------|--------------|
| Where | are | you | from? |
| Why | are | we | here? |
| Who | is | that girl? | |
| When | is | your appointment? | |
| What | am | I | for Halloween? |
| How | are | you? | |

Common Mistake: *Where you from?*

Although this may be fine in very informal spoken English, it is not Ok in written English. There must always be a verb, in every sentence and in every question. This mistake comes from the question spoken with the contraction, *"Where're you from?"* in which the contraction ('re) is almost not heard.

Exercise 4:

Directions: Make questions using the following words and adding the correct form of the 'be' verb. Make sure you use the correct format:

[*Wh word + be verb + subject + complement*]

Example: (you from/ where)

Answer: *Where are you from?*

1. (What/that)
2. (Who/she)
3. (Where/my pants)
4. (When/you/at home)
5. (Why /I /here)
6. (How/ your cousins)
7. (Why/ you/ on the phone)

*Rule 5: (This/That/These/Those) 'This' is to identify a singular object that is near and that you can touch. 'These' is used to identify plural objects that are near and that you can touch. 'That' is used to identify a singular object that is far away and that you have to point to. 'Those' is used to identify plural objects that are far away and that you have to point to.* (Use the table as a reference)

|      | Singular | Plural |
|------|----------|--------|
| Near | This     | These  |
| Far  | That     | Those  |

Examples:

- *This is* a nice house. (You are inside the house)
- *That is* a nice house. (You are outside of the house, pointing to a house)
- *These are* my friends. (Your friends are close.)
- *Those are* my friends. (Your friends are far. You have to point to them with your finger)

Exercise 5:

Directions: Fill in the blank with the correct term (this, that, those, these)

Example: _____ is a great party. (You are at the party)

Answer: .........*This*.........is a great party.

1. Can you see a girl over there with black pants and a blue shirt? _____ is my sister.
2. I want you to meet my friend. Susan, _____ is Sara. Sara, this is Susan.

3. _____ are my friends. This is Sara. This is Maria. This is Mike.
4. Can you see two big dogs across the street? _____ are my dogs.


Other Things to Note: Contractions

In spoken English especially, contractions are used. Contractions are fine in written English as well, but if you are writing a formal essay, letter, or any other formal type of writing, avoid using them. Use the following table as a reference.

| Formal | Contraction (affirmative) | Contraction (negative) |
|--------|---------------------------|------------------------|
| I am | I'm | I'm not |
| You are | You're | You're not/ You aren't |
| He is | He's | He's not/ He isn't |
| She is | She's | She's not/ She isn't |
| They are | They're | They're not/ They aren't |
| We are | We're | We're not/ We aren't |
| It is | It's | It's not/ It isn't |

*After checking your answers, if you think you need more practice with the 'be' verb, continue on to the additional exercises, which I would recommend doing before continuing onto the next chapter. Otherwise, let's move onto Chapter 3.

## Answers to Exercises in Chapter 2

Answers to "Check your Knowledge"

1. ~~I from~~ San Francisco. I *am* from San Francisco.
2. Where ~~you are~~ from? Where *are you* from?
3. She ~~is come~~ to the party. She *is coming* to the party. /She *comes* to the party.
4. ~~Everything is~~ Ok? *Is everything* Ok?
5. ~~His not~~ here right now. *He's not* here right now.

Answers to Exercise 1:

1. They ….. are …… happy.
2. She ….. is …… on the phone.
3. My computer …..is…… broken.
4. I ….. am…… sure.
5. Her name …..is….. Sarah.
6. My father and I ……are….. on vacation.
7. My friend Charlie …..is…… lost.
8. We …..are….. in the library.
9. My shoes …..are….. dirty.
10. My shoe …..is….. clean.

Answers to Exercise 2:

1. My brothers …..are not/ aren't….. here.
2. The cat ……is not/ isn't….. sick.
3. Sarah and I …..are not / arent'…..at the park anymore.
4. The store ……is not/ isn't…. crowded right now.
5. My sister …… is not / isn't …… married.
6. I …. am not/ 'm not…. a doctor.

Answers to Exercise 3:

1. Is my brother at home?
2. Are they sick?
3. Is the computer expensive?
4. Is it hot today?
5. Are the waves good?
6. Am I in trouble?
7. Are we late?
8. Are your friends nice?

Answers to Exercise 4:

1. What is that?
2. Who is she?
3. Where are my pants?
4. When are you at home?
5. Why am I here?
6. How are your cousins?
7. Why are you on the phone?

Answers to Exercise 5:

1. Can you see a girl over there with black pants and a blue shirt? .....That..... is my sister.
2. I want you to meet my friend. Susan, ....this.... is Sara. Sara .....this .......is Susan.
3. .....These..... are my friends. This is Sara. This is Maria. This is Mike.
4. Can you see two big dogs across the street? ......Those..... are my dogs.

## Chapter 2: Additional Exercises

Do the following exercises and check your answers before taking the Chapter 2 quiz.

Exercise 6: Dialogue Fill in the Blank

Directions: Read the following dialogue and fill in the blank with the words from the box. Two words in the box will not be used. You can use each word more than once.

| is | am | are | that | this | 'm not | those |
|----|----|----|------|------|--------|-------|

A: Hi, my name _____ Andrea. What _____ your name?

B: I _____ Bobby. Nice to meet you Andrea. Where _____ you from?

A: California, but my parents _____ from Mexico. Any you?

B: I _____ from New York.

A: How old _____ you?

B: I _____ 23 years old, but my birthday _____ next week and then I'll be 24.

A: Nice. I _____ 23 also. _____ you a student?

B: No, I _____. I _____ an engineer. What about you?

A: I'm a student here. My sister _____ a student here too. _____'s her over there.

B: _____ she older than you?

A: No, she _____ younger. _____ those your books?

B: Yes, they are. _____ the library open? I need to return some books.

A: Yes, it _____. I'll go with you.

Exercise 7: Find the Error

Directions: Each sentence has a mistake. Identify the error and correct the sentence.

1. They are at the park?
2. That girls across the street are not students.
3. His not here right now.
4. We is not at home.
5. Who she is?
6. Are you happy? Yes, I'm.
7. Is he sick? No, he is.

Exercise 8

Directions: Use the words below to make questions using the "be" verb. Then, answer the questions, or practice asking and answering the questions with a partner.

Example: Name?

Answer: What is your name? (My name is…)

1. Name?
2. From?
3. Nationality?
4. Age?
5. Married?
6. Single?
7. A student?
8. your job?

Exercise 9:

Directions: Write your answers to the questions, or practice the questions by asking someone else.

1. Are you happy?
2. Are your parents still married?
3. Are you single?
4. Are you hungry?
5. Are you thirsty?
6. Is your mother at home?
7. Is your father at work?
8. Are you usually late or early?
9. Are you from the United States?
10. Is English your native language?
11. Is English easy for you?
12. Am I a good friend?
13. Are we inside or outside?
14. What is your native language?
15. What sports are you interested in?
16. What is your job?
17. What is your favorite food?
18. What is your favorite holiday?
19. Who is your best friend?
20. Who are your parents?
21. Who is your favorite actor?
22. Who am I?

23. Where am I?
24. Where are you?
25. Where is your family?
26. Where is your favorite restaurant?
27. When are you the most alert?
28. When is your birthday?
29. Why are you here?
30. Why are the plants green?
31. Why is gas so expensive?
32. Why are so many people overweight?
33. How old are you?
34. How old is your mother?
35. How old is your father?
36. How are you?
37. How is your family?
38. How is the food here?
39. How much is a cup of coffee (where you're from)?
40. How many children are there in your family?


Chapter 2 Quiz


Directions: Fill in the blank with the correct form of the "be" verb.

1. He _____ not here right now.
2. We _____ students at this university.
3. _____ I late?
4. Those girls _____ not part of my group.
5. That computer _____ expensive.


Directions: Choose the best answer

6. You _____ at home. You're at the supermarket. (isn't/ aren't/ am not)
7. She _____ a cashier. She's a nurse. (isn't/ aren't/ am not)
8. They _____ in the store. They are at the bank. (isn't/ aren't/ am not)
9. The supermarket _____ crowded. It's empty. (isn't / aren't/ am not)
10. I'm _____ sure about the answer. I don't know. (isn't/ not/ aren't)


Directions: Choose the correct answer

11. The machines (is/ are) empty.
12. (This/ These) blanket is clean.

13. (They/ They're) on sale.
14. The (towel/ towels) are dirty.
15. (That/ Those) students are new.

Directions: Identify the adjective in each sentence.

16. The parking lot is empty.
17. The store isn't crowded.
18. The samples are free.
19. Those are nice cars.
20. San Diego is hot today.

Directions: Use the following words to create questions using the 'be' verb

21. (you/ hungry)
22. (how old/ he)
23. (what/ that)
24. (where /my shoes)
25. (when/ their birthdays)

Answers to Chapter 2 Additional Exercises

Answers to Exercise 6:

A: Hi, my name ........is......... Andrea. What .......is........your name?

B: I .........am....... Bobby. Nice to meet you Andrea. Where ...........are........... you from?

A: California, but my parents ..........are............ from Mexico. Any you?

B: I .........am......... from New York.

A: How old ...........are............ you?

B: I .........am......... 23 years old, but my birthday ..........is.............. next week and then I'll be 24.

A: Nice. I ............am........... 23 also. ..............Are.................. you a student?

B: No, I .....'m not.............. I ...............am.............. an engineer. What about you?

A: I'm a student here. My sister ..................is .................a student here too. .....That.....'s her over there.

B: ...............Is...........she older than you?

A: No, she ..........is............ younger. ...........Are.............. those your books?

B: Yes, they are.  ............Is.............. the library open? I need to return some books.

A: Yes, it ..........is........... I'll go with you.


Answers to Exercise 7:

1. ~~They are~~ at the park?  *Are they* at the park?
2. ~~That~~ girls across the street are not students. *Those girls* across the street are not students.
3. ~~His~~ not here right now. *He's* (or, He is) not here right now.
4. ~~We is~~ not at home. *We are* not at home.
5. Who ~~she is~~? Who *is she*?
6. Are you happy? Yes, ~~I'm~~. Yes, *I am*. (no contractions in the "Yes" short answers)
7. Is he sick? No, ~~he is~~. No, he *isn't*.


Answers to Exercise 8:

1. Name? *What is your name? (My name is. . .)*
2. From? *Where are you from? (I'm from. . .)*
3. Nationality? *What is your nationality? (My nationality is. . .)*
4. Age? *How old are you? (I am. . . years old)*
5. Married? *Are you married? (Yes, I am. /No, I'm not.)*
6. Single? *Are you single? (Yes, I am. /No, I'm not.)*

7. A student? Are you a student? (Yes, I am. / No, I'm not.)
8. your job? What is your job? (I'm a . . .)


Answers to Chapter 2 Quiz:

1. He ….is….. not here right now.
2. We ….are….. students at this university.
3. ….Am…. I late?
4. Those girls …..are….. not part of my group.
5. That computer …….is……. expensive.

6. aren't
7. isn't
8. aren't
9. isn't
10. not

11. The machines are empty.
12. This blanket is clean.
13. They're on sale.
14. The towels are dirty.
15. Those students are new.

16. The parking lot is *empty*. (Remember, adjectives come after the "be" verb, or before a noun)
17. The store isn't *crowded*.
18. The samples are *free*.
19. Those are *nice* cars.
20. San Diego is *hot* today.

21. (you/ hungry) Are you hungry?
22. (how old/ he) How old is he?
23. (what/ that) What is that?
24. (where /my shoes) Where are my shoes?
25. (when/ their birthdays) When are their birthdays?

# Chapter 3: The Apostrophe ('s)

*Rule 1: Possessive adjectives (my, his, your, our, etc.) come before a noun (N) to show possession. Don't confuse possessive adjectives (PA) with subject pronouns (SP), which come before a verb (V). In other words:*

[PA + N] / [SP + V]

See the following charts:

| Subject Pronoun | Possessive Adj. |
|---|---|
| I | My |
| You | Your |
| He | His |
| She | Her |
| It | Its |
| They | Their |
| We | Our |

[SP + V]

| Subject Pronoun | Verb | (complement) |
|---|---|---|
| I | am | here. |
| You | have | a lot of friends. |
| He | needs | more time. |
| She | lives | over there. |
| It | is | difficult. |
| They | are | at the park. |
| We | found | him. |

[PA + N]

| Possessive Adj. | Noun | Verb | Complement |
|---|---|---|---|
| My | computer | is | expensive. |
| Your | children | aren't | here. |
| His | birthday | is | next week. |
| Its | eyes | are | small. |
| Her | father | lives | next door. |
| Their | house | has | four bedrooms. |
| Our | family | is getting | bigger. |

**Common Mistake 1:** *Their not here right now. /There not here right now.*

"Their" is a possessive adjective and should only go before a noun (their car). "They're not here right now" is the proper sentence, since "They're" means "They are". "There" refers to a place and is similar in both spelling and meaning to the word "here".

Common Mistake 2: *Its cold outside. / My cat doesn't want to eat it's food.*

*It's = it is*, and *"its"* without an apostrophe ('s) is to show possession, and is similar to the words *their, his, her*. The first sentence should be: *It's cold outside* (since *it is* cold outside). The second sentence should be: My cat doesn't want to eat *its* food (the food belongs to the cat; it shows possession).

Exercise 1

Directions: Choose the best answer for each sentence.

1. (I/My) sister is sick.
2. (He/His) car is black.
3. (She/Her) TV is broken.
4. (They/Their) are not here today.
5. (You/Your) house is big.
6. (We/Our) children are late.
7. (You're/Your) on time.
8. (They're/Their) students.
9. (He's/His) paper is finished.
10. (I'm/My) busy.

*Rule 2: Add an apostrophe + s ('s) to a noun to show ownership or that something belongs to someone. An ('s) can take the place of its, his, her, their. A noun with an ('s) at the end is called a possessive noun. Notice that possessive nouns always come before another noun.*

- Example 1: *Peter's* house is blue.
- Example 2: The *cat's* food is not here.
- Example 3: Can you talk to *Mike's* father?
- Example 4: I want to meet *Sara's* husband.
- Example 5: Her *sister's* name is Helen.

*Rule 3: If the possessive noun is plural and already ends with the letter (s), just put an apostrophe (') without adding an (s).*

- My *students'* tests are finished.
- His *parents'* car drives fast.

Notice the difference between these two sentences:

- The *cat's* food is not here. (There is only one cat)
- The *cats'* food is not here. (There is more than one cat)


Exercise 2:

Directions: Rewrite the sentence to include a possessive noun with an ('s) or an (')

Example: The brother of Sara is at the park.

Answer: *Sara's* brother is at the park.

1. The husband of my best friend is American.
2. I want to buy the computer of my friend.
3. The soup of this restaurant is delicious.
4. This is the house of my parents.
5. That is the dog of my friend Eric.
6. The books of the students are expensive.


*Rule 4: Besides possession, an ('s) can also be the contraction for "is" or "has".*


| Example Sentence | Meaning of the ('s) |
|---|---|
| He's not here right now. | He's = He is |
| She's never been to Canada. | She's = She has |
| Sara's computer is broken. | Sara's = Her computer |
| It's difficult. | It's = It is |
| My brothers' TV doesn't work. | brothers' = their TV |
| I can't find my brother's keys. | brother's = his keys |


Exercise 3: For each sentence, Identify the meaning of the ('s) as in the chart above.

| Sentence | Meaning of the ('s) |
|---|---|
| 1. She's always on time | |
| 2. We can't find Susan's purse. | |
| 3. Where is your father's car? | |
| 4. My daughter's grades are great. | |
| 5. Sara's at work right now. | |
| 6. The internet's slow. | |

| 7. His friends' houses don't have room. | |
|---|---|

*Rule 5: Don't put an ('s) on plural nouns that do not show possession.*

- Incorrect: My *parent's* have a lot of free time. (parents = plural noun)
- Correct: My *parents* have a lot of free time.

In this sentence, the word "parents" does not show possession and the letter (s) is used to indicate a plural noun. It is not a contraction for "is" or "has"

The only reasons to put an ('s) is if:

(1) it has the same meaning as *his/her/its/their* to show possession, or
(2) the ('s) is the contraction for "is" or "has"

Exercise 4: Decide if the following sentences are correct or incorrect.

1. I can't find my turtle's.
2. Sara's garden has a lot of vegetables.
3. Her children's behavior is horrible.
4. My sister drive's like a crazy person.
5. All the surfboard's that I have are old.

Answers to Exercises Chapter 3

Exercise 1:

1. (I/*My*) sister is sick.
2. (He/*His*) car is black.
3. (She/*Her*) TV is broken.
4. (*They*/Their) are not here today.
5. (You/*Your*) house is big.
6. (We/*Our*) children are late.
7. (*You're*/Your) on time.
8. (*They're*/Their) students.
9. (He's/*His*) paper is finished.
10. (*I'm*/My) busy.

Exercise 2:

1. The husband of my best friend is American. *My best friend's husband is American.*
2. I want to buy the computer of my friend. *I want to buy my friend's computer.*
3. The soup of this restaurant is delicious. *This restaurant's soup is delicious.*
4. This is the house of my parents. *This is my parents' house.*
5. That is the dog of my friend Eric. *That is my friend Eric's dog.*
6. The books of the students are expensive. *The students' books are expensive.*

Exercise 3:

| Sentence | Meaning of the ('s) |
|---|---|
| 1. She's always on time | she's = She is |
| 2. We can't find Susan's purse. | Susan's = her (purse) |
| 3. Where is your father's car? | father's = his (car) |
| 4. My daughter's grades are great. | daughter's = her (grades) |
| 5. Sara's at work right now. | Sara's = Sara is |
| 6. The internet's slow. | internet's = internet is |
| 7. His friends' houses don't have room. | friends' = their (houses) |

Exercise 4:

1. I can't find my turtle's. Incorrect ("turtles" is just a plural noun)
2. Sara's garden has a lot of vegetables. Correct (her garden)

3. Her children's behavior is horrible. Correct (their behavior)
4. My sister drive's like a crazy person. Incorrect ("drives" is a verb)
5. All the surfboard's that I have are old. Incorrect ("surfboards" is just a plural noun)

After checking your answers, if you think you need more practice with this grammar topic, continue on to the additional exercises, which I would recommend doing before continuing onto the next chapter. Otherwise, let's move onto Chapter 4.

## Chapter 3 Additional Exercises

Exercise 5: Dialogue

Directions: The following dialogue is missing a number of apostrophes ('s). Add in the missing apostrophes (').

A: Hey Mike! I found your brothers phone in Saras car.

B: Oh really? Give me Mikes phone and I'll give it to him when I go to my moms house.

A: Ok. So whats for dinner?

B: I'm not sure. My sisters kids will be there so probably something that they like.

A: Ok. I'm going to Saras house after my classes to have dinner there. I think we're going to make tacos. My cousins will be there too.

B: Is your cousin Christina coming? I have her videos that she let me borrow.

A: Yeah. You can bring those to Saras place.

B: Ok, sounds good. I'll see you later.


Exercise 6: Possessive Nouns

Directions: Rewrite the following paragraph to contain as many possessive nouns with ('s) as possible. The first change is done for you.

Example: *Sara's husband's name is Jack.*

This is Sara. Her husband is here. His name is Jack. Their house is for sale. Its neighborhood is full of families. Their children are happy to move. His parents are going to help them move. They are moving to the smallest state in the United States, Rhode Island. The friends of their children are sad to say goodbye. Jack has a new job. Its salary and benefits are much better than his old job.


Exercise 7: Discussion questions with Possessives

Directions: Write down your answers to the following questions, or find a partner to discuss the questions with.

1. What's your father's name?
2. What's your mother's name?
3. How are your neighborhood's restaurants?
4. What is the name of your country's president?
5. What do you think of your country's food?
6. What do you think of your parents' house?
7. Do you miss your mother's cooking?

8. What do you do on New Year's Day?
9. Are you satisfied with your job's salary?
10. Why are students' university books so expensive?
11. Who is your favorite movie's main actor?

Chapter 3 Quiz:

Directions: Rewrite each sentence to include an ('s).

1. The father of my best friend is in jail.
2. The desk of my English teacher is a mess.
3. I want to eat the homemade pizza of my mother.
4. I miss the yoga studio of my old neighborhood.
5. She is the girlfriend of my cousin.

Directions: Decide if the sentences are correct or incorrect

6. Manals boyfriend forgot her birthday.
7. Susan always comes home for her mother's cooking.
8. My computer's keyboard isn't working.
9. The United State's largest state is Alaska.
10. My sister's friends usually drive her to work.
11. My cousin change's her plan all the time.
12. I can't watch horror movies.
13. The dogs foot is hurt.
14. My cell phone's alarm clock doesn't work.
15. My team lost the tournaments final match.

Answers to Additional Exercises Chapter 3

Exercise 5: Dialogue

A: Hey Mike! I found your *brother's* phone in *Sara's* car.

B: Oh really? Give me *Mike's* phone and I'll give it to him when I go to my *mom's* house.

A: Ok. So *what's* for dinner?

B: I'm not sure. My *sister's* kids will be there so probably something that they like.

A: Ok. I'm going to *Sara's* house after my classes to have dinner there. I think we're going to make tacos. My cousins will be there too.

B: Is your cousin Christina coming? I have her videos that she let me borrow.

A: Yeah. You can bring those to *Sara's* place.

B: Ok, sounds good. I'll see you later.


Exercise 6: Answers may vary

Sample Answer: Sara's husband's name is Jack. Sara and Jack's house is for sale. The house's neighborhood is full of families. Sara and Jack's children are happy to move. Jack's parents are going to help them move. They are moving to the United States' smallest state, Rhode Island. Sara and Jack's children's friends are sad to say goodbye. Jack's new job's salary and benefits are much better than Jack's old job.

Original: This is Sara. Her husband is here. His name is Jack. Their house is for sale. Its neighborhood is full of families. Their children are happy to move. His parents are going to help them move. They are moving to the smallest state in the United States, Rhode Island. The friends of their children are sad to say goodbye. Jack has a new job. Its salary and benefits are much better than his old job.


Answers to Chapter 3 Quiz:

1. The father of my best friend is in jail. My best friend's father is in jail.
2. The desk of my English teacher is a mess. My English teacher's desk is a mess.
3. I want to eat the homemade pizza of my mother. I want to eat my mother's homemade pizza.
4. I miss the yoga studio of my old neighborhood. I miss my old neighborhood's yoga studio.
5. She is the girlfriend of my cousin. She is my cousin's girlfriend.

6. Manals boyfriend forgot her birthday. Incorrect (Manal's boyfriend)
7. Susan always comes home for her mother's cooking. Correct
8. My computer's keyboard isn't working. Correct
9. The United State's largest state is Alaska. Incorrect (The United States' largest state)

10. My sister's friends usually drive her to work. Correct
11. My cousin change's her plan all the time. Incorrect (My cousin changes—verb)
12. I can't watch horror movies. Correct
13. The dogs foot is hurt. Incorrect (The dog's foot is hurt)
14. My cell phone's alarm clock doesn't work. Correct
15. My team lost the tournaments final match. Incorrect (the tournament's final match)

# Chapter 4: Articles (A, An, The)

Before we get into the rules, take a look at some basic concepts that are important to know when learning about articles.

1. There are two types of articles: Indefinite articles (*a, an*) and the definite article (*the*)

2. Nouns can be *singular*, meaning only one, or *plural*, meaning more than one

   o Singular: person, friend, egg, minute
   o Plural: people, friends, eggs, minutes

3. Nouns can also be either countable, or non-countable nouns. Countable nouns, or count nouns are those which you can count (people, friends, eggs, minutes, etc.) If you can put a number in front of the noun (5 people, 6 friends, 2 eggs, 5 minutes), then it is a countable noun. Non-countable nouns are nouns which we cannot count. They can never be made plural or have the letter 's' at the end. Some examples include: information, homework, coffee, water, advice, etc. If we cannot put a number in front of the noun, or if it sounds strange (2 informations, 3 homeworks), it is a non-countable noun.

*Rule 1: Use the indefinite article (a, an) before a singular countable noun.*

| Example | Singular countable nouns |
|---|---|
| I am *a* teacher at *a* local elementary school. | teacher, school |
| We are at *a* beach in Thailand. | beach |
| She has *a* difficult job. | job |
| She has *a* daughter. | daughter |

Note that if an adjective comes before a noun (difficult job), the article goes before the adjective:

(*a* difficult *job*).

*Rule 2: Use the indefinite article 'an' instead of 'a' before singular countable nouns, or noun phrases that begin with a vowel sound (a, e, i, o, u).*

| Example | Singular countable nouns that begin with a vowel sound |
|---|---|
| Can you give me an apple? | apple |
| There is an elephant in the zoo. | elephant |
| My mother's friend has an illness. | illness |

| | |
|---|---|
| She always gives them an easy test. | easy test (*easy* is an adjective, but *easy test* is a noun phrase) |
| My father is an old man. | old man ( noun phrase) |
| Do you have an umbrella? | umbrella |

Exercise 1

Directions: Fill in the blank with '*a*', '*an*', or nothing (*X*) if the sentence doesn't need an article.

1. She has _____ older brother.
2. My sister needs _____ money.
3. Can I have _____ cup of coffee?
4. They have _____ dog, _____ cat, and _____ turtles.
5. Are you _____ hard worker?
6. My brother is _____ engineer.

*Rule 3: Never use the indefinite article (a, an) before an uncountable noun*

| *Example* | *Non-countable noun* |
|---|---|
| I have some information for you. | information |
| She wants me to give her some advice. | advice |
| Do you have some water? | water |
| She always has homework. | homework |

- Note: The word "some" is often used in front of non-countable nouns

Here's a list of other common non-countable nouns:

| *Abstractions* | *Activities* | *Food* | *Liquids* | *Natural Events* | *Groups of Similar Items* |
|---|---|---|---|---|---|
| happiness | homework | meat | Coffee | weather | mail |
| fun | chess | bread | Water | rain | luggage |
| honesty | housework | butter | Blood | electricity | clothing |
| enjoyment | music | fish | gasoline | snow | furniture |
| information | reading | chicken | oil | sunshine | equipment |
| knowledge | sleeping | popcorn | soup | heat | money |
| intelligence | soccer | cheese | wine | humidity | software |

Exercise 2

Directions: Fill in the blank with '*a*', '*an*', or nothing (*X*) if the sentence doesn't need an article

1. _____ Life is not always easy.
2. My father is _____ nice person.

3. You need to eat _____ vegetables.
4. I love listening to _____ music.
5. Her yard has _____ avocado trees, _____ red flowers and _____ vegetable garden.
6. Can you give me _____ advice?
7. It's _____ good opportunity.
8. She always has _____ bread with her dinner.
9. I need to buy _____ umbrella.
10. The food is _____delicious.

*Rule 4: Use the definite article (the) before any noun (singular, plural, countable, non-countable) that has already been identified. This means that both the speaker and the listener know which noun is being discussed; they are referring to a specific noun and not speaking in general.*

| Example | Explanation |
|---|---|
| Where is *the book* that I gave you? | The book is identified; the speaker is talking about a specific book (the one I gave you). |
| *The teacher* gave a lot of homework. | The teacher is identified; both the speaker and listener know which teacher is being discussed. |
| I need to pick *the kids* up from school. | The kids are identified. The speaker isn't going to pick up any kids, but a specific group of kids. |
| *The milk* is bad. | Not just any milk from anywhere, but the milk that is in the refrigerator |
| *The clothes* are expensive there. | Not all clothes in general, but the particular clothes (in that store) are expensive. |

Compare the following examples:

| Indefinite Article (a, an) | Definite Article (the) | Explanation |
|---|---|---|
| We killed *a bear*. | We killed *the bear*. | The first example (a bear) shows that one bear was killed and that there are possibly more bears. The second example shows that there was only one bear, and now there are no more. |
| Can I have *an apple*? | Can I have *the apple*? | The first example (an apple) asks for any apple in general and indicates that there are more than one apple. The second example (the apple) indicates one specific apple. |

Exercise 3

Directions: Fill in the blank with '*a*', '*an*', '*the*', or nothing (*X*) if the sentence doesn't need an article

1. I have _____ friend I want to introduce you to.

2. _____ Happiness is something that everybody wants.
3. I was absent today. Did _____ teacher give _____ homework?
4. Let's go to _____ restaurant. I don't have any food to cook.
5. I need to buy _____ milk.
6. _____ coffee that your mother makes is so good.
7. I would like to have _____ American friend to practice _____ English with.
8. What is _____ answer to question number six?
9. Be careful. There are _____ snakes here.
10. You need to take _____ picture of _____ elephant for the magazine.

## Answers to Chapter 4 Exercises

### Exercise 1:

1. She has ……an…… older brother. (*brother* is a singular count noun; *older* begins with a vowel sound)
2. My sister needs ……..X…….. money. (*money* is an uncountable noun)
3. Can I have ……a…….. cup of coffee? (*cup* is a singular count noun)
4. They have …..a…… dog, …….a….. cat, and ….X…. turtles. (*dog* and *cat* are singular count nouns, and *turtles* is a plural noun)
5. Are you ….a….. hard worker? (*worker* is a singular count noun)
6. My brother is ….an…. engineer. (*engineer* is a singular count noun that begins with a vowel sound)

### Exercise 2:

1. …….X…… Life is not always easy. (In this sentence *Life* is an abstract noun and uncountable)
2. My father is …..a….. nice person. (*person* is a singular count noun)
3. You need to eat ………X……… vegetables. (*vegetables* is plural)
4. I love listening to ….X…… music. (*music* is an uncountable noun)
5. Her yard has ……X……avocado trees, ……X……. red flowers and …….a……vegetable garden. (*garden* is a singular count noun; *trees* and *flowers* are plural nouns)
6. Can you give me ……..X…… advice? (*advice* is an uncountable noun)
7. It's ……a……… good opportunity. (*opportunity* is a singular count noun)
8. She always has ……X…..bread with her dinner. (*bread* is an uncountable noun)
9. I need to buy …….an…….umbrella. (*umbrella* is a singular count noun that begins with a vowel sound)
10. The food is …….X……..delicious. (*delicious* is an adjective)

### Exercise 3:

1. I have ….a…. friend I want to introduce you to. (*Friend* is a singular count noun. The friend is not identified)
2. ……X…… Happiness is something that everybody wants. (*Happiness* is an abstract noun and therefore uncountable. It's also talking about happiness in general)
3. I was absent today. Did ….the…. teacher give ….X….. homework? (*The teacher* is identified—both the speaker and listener know which teacher. *Homework* is an uncountable noun and not identified. They are talking about homework in general)
4. Let's go to ……a/ the….. restaurant. I don't have any food to cook. (Both answers are possible since it's not clear if the speaker is talking about a specific restaurant or any restaurant in general)
5. I need to buy ……..X…… milk. (*Milk* is an uncountable noun and the speaker is talking about milk in general, not specifically)

6. ......The.... coffee that your mother makes is so good. (the coffee is identified specifically with the phrase "that your mother makes")
7. I would like to have .....an.... American friend to practice ....X.... English with. (*friend* is a singular count noun; *English* is an uncountable noun)
8. What is .....the.... answer to question number six? (there is only one answer; the speaker wants a specific answer, not any answer in general)
9. Be careful. There are ....X..... snakes here. (snakes is a plural count noun; snakes in general, not any specific snakes)
10. You need to take ....a... picture of .....an/ the.... elephant for the magazine. (picture is a singular count noun; it's not clear if the picture is for a specific identified elephant, or for any elephant in general, so both answers are possible)

After checking your answers, if you think you need more practice with the articles, continue on to the additional exercises, which I would recommend doing before continuing onto the next chapter. Otherwise, let's move onto Chapter 5.

Exercise 4: Dialogue

Directions: fill in the blanks of the dialogue with *a, an, the*, or *X* (if no article is needed)

A: Mike, there's _____ spider on your head.

B: What? Get it off!

A: _____ spider is small. Just take it off yourself.

B: I have _____ fear of _____ spiders. Will you please take it off for me?

A: All right. Hold still. _____ spider is more afraid than you are.

B: Is it gone?

A: Yes, I got it.

B: Thanks. That was scary.

A: Whatever. I'm hungry. Do you want to have _____ lunch with me?

B: Sure. I would love _____ hamburger.

A: _____ hamburgers at Jimbo's are really good. Do you want to go there?

B: Yeah, sounds good.

A: How did you do on Mr. Smith's math test?

B: I got _____ A. It was _____ easy test. You?

A: I got _____ B. _____ second part was hard for me.

B: I'll show you my test and we can talk about it.


Exercise 5: Find the Mistakes

Directions: The following paragraph has six mistakes regarding article usage. See if you can identify the mistakes.

Today is beautiful day in San Diego. A sky is blue and the sun is shining. This is how most days in San Diego are. A weather here is so lovely. Even in the winter, there are sunny and warm days that allow people to go to beaches. However, having beautiful weather all the time has its drawbacks. Sometimes you need to study or get some work done, but this becomes difficult when it's so beautiful outside. On the days that I have to study or work all the day, I secretly hope for a rain and thunderstorms so that it goes with my mood.

Chapter 4 Quiz

Directions: Decide if the following nouns are count or uncountable

1. fruit
2. chair
3. information
4. computer
5. advice
6. homework
7. money
8. garden
9. dollar
10. tea

Directions: Fill in the blanks with *a, an, the*, or *X* if no article is needed

11. He's _____ old man.
12. _____ necklaces that he makes are amazing.
13. Would you like _____ glass of water?
14. All _____ people need _____ love in their life.
15. My sister works as _____ architect in _____ building behind the gas station.
16. _____ money is very important in _____ life.
17. _____ woman came to see you yesterday when you were gone, but I don't know who she is.
18. _____ woman I met at the party came here yesterday.
19. I want to put _____ garden in my backyard.
20. _____ people that live next door are noisy and rude.

Answers to Additional Exercises Chapter 4

Exercise 4: Dialogue

A: Mike, there's ….a….. spider on your head.

B: What? Get it off!

A: …..The…. spider is small. Just take it off yourself.

B: I have …..a….. fear of …..X…..spiders. Will you please take it off for me?

A: All right. Hold still. …..The….. spider is more afraid than you are.

B: Is it gone?

A: Yes, I got it.

B: Thanks. That was scary.

A: Whatever. I'm hungry. Do you want to have ….X….. lunch with me?

B: Sure. I would love ……a……. hamburger.

A: ……The….. hamburgers at Jimbo's are really good. Do you want to go there?

B: Yeah, sounds good.

A: How did you do on Mr. Smith's math test?

B: I got …..an…. A. It was ……an…. easy test. You?

A: I got …..a….. B. …..The….. second part was hard for me.

B: I'll show you my test and we can talk about it.

Exercise 5: Find the Mistakes

Today is a (1) beautiful day in San Diego. The (2) sky is blue and the sun is shining. This is how most days in San Diego are. The (3) weather here is so lovely. Even in the winter, there are sunny and warm days that allow people to go to the (4) beaches. However, having beautiful weather all the time has its drawbacks. Sometimes you need to study or get some work done, but this becomes difficult when it's so beautiful outside. On the days that I have to study or work all day (5), I secretly hope for rain (6) and thunderstorms so that it goes with my mood.

> Explanations:
>    1. "day" is a singular count noun, so we must say "a beautiful day"
>    2. We are talking about the San Diego sky
>    3. We're talking specifically about the weather in San Diego, not just the weather in general
>    4. We're talking specifically about the beaches of San Diego
>    5. "all day" is a fixed expression. We never say "all the day" in English

6. rain is an uncountable noun

Chapter 4 Quiz:

1. fruit (uncountable)
2. chair (count)
3. information (uncountable)
4. computer (count)
5. advice (uncountable)
6. homework (uncountable)
7. money (uncountable)
8. garden (count)
9. dollar (uncountable)
10. tea (uncountable)

11. He's ....an.... old man.
12. .....The.... necklaces that he makes are amazing.
13. Would you like ....a...... glass of water?
14. All ......X...... people need .....X....... love in their life.
15. My sister works as ......an..... architect in .....the.... building behind the gas station.
16. ......X..... money is very important in .......X..... life.
17. .......A...... woman came to see you yesterday when you were gone, but I don't know who she is.
18. ........The.... woman I met at the party came here yesterday.
19. I want to put .....a..... garden in my backyard.
20. ......The..... people that live next door are noisy and rude.

# Chapter 5: The Present Simple Tense (What does she do?)

In the present simple tense, there are two types of verbs:

1. The 'be' verb (am, is, are)
2. All other verbs (sleep, eat, listen, speak, swim, think)

The first four rules apply only to type 2 (all other verbs). We already covered the 'be' verb in Chapter 2, but the rules at the end of this chapter are to make sure you don't confuse the grammar rules that apply to the 'be' verb with the grammar rules that apply to all the other verbs.

*Rule 1: In the present simple tense, the verb only changes when the subject is He, She, or It, also known as third person singular. When the subject is He, She, or It, you must add an (-s) to the end of the verb.*

See the chart below:

| Subject | Verb (to know) |
|---------|----------------|
| I | know |
| You | know |
| He | *knows* |
| She | *knows* |
| It | *knows* |
| They | know |
| We | know |

Note: Some verbs are irregular, meaning that you may need to change the spelling of the verb, or add the letters (*es*) when you put it in the third person singular. For example: *I go, she goes/ I have, he has/ I do, she does, etc.*

Exercise 1:

Directions: Fill in the blank with the correct form of the verb in the present simple tense. Make sure to add (s) to the verb if the subject is third person singular (he, she, it).

Example: Elizabeth _____ in California. (live)

Answer: Elizabeth..........*lives*......................... in California.

1. We _____ the answer. (know)
2. Mr. Roberts _____ two cars. (have)
3. My computer _____ very well. (work)
4. I _____ breakfast every morning at 8:00. (eat)
5. The students _____ more books. (need)

6. This student _____ another book. (want)
7. Those girls _____ home at 4:00. (go)
8. My brother _____ home at 2:00. (go)
9. We _____ our homework at 8:00. (do)
10. My mom always _____ me the truth. (tell)

*Rule 2: In the negative form of the present simple tense, you add do not (don't) or does not (doesn't) before the base form of the verb. The subjects I, You, They, We use "do not" before the verb (ex: I do not know). The subjects He, She, and It use "does not" before the verb (ex: She does not know.) Never add an (s) to the verb in the negative form.* **See the chart below:**

| Subject | Negative Verb (to know) | Contraction |
|---------|-------------------------|-------------|
| I | do not know | I *don't* know |
| You | do not know | You *don't* know |
| He | *does* not know | He *doesn't* know |
| She | *does* not know | She *doesn't* know |
| It | *does* not know | It *doesn't* know |
| They | do not know | They *don't* know |
| We | do not know | We *don't* know |

**Common Mistake:** *She have it. /She don't have it.*

Since the subject is "she", we obviously need to say: *She has it. /She doesn't have it.*

Exercise 2

Directions: Fill in the blank with the negative form of the present simple tense.

Example: She _____ the truth. (know)

Answer: She .........*doesn't know*.................... the truth.

1. Mr. Smith _____ breakfast. (eat)
2. The students _____ their homework. (understand)
3. My sister _____ her food. (like)
4. My computer _____. (work)
5. The stores _____ meat. (sell)
6. My coffee _____ sugar. (have)
7. These tables _____ a lot. (cost)
8. That table _____ a lot. (cost)
9. They _____ cigarettes. (smoke)

10. We _____ to school on Fridays. (go)


*Rule 3: To make Yes/No questions in the present simple tense, follow the format:*

*[Do/Does + Subject + Base Verb + (complement)]*

*Base Verb = the basic form of the verb, without adding the letter (s), (-ing) or putting (to) in front

| Do/Does | Subject | Base Verb | (complement) |
|---------|---------|-----------|--------------|
| Do | you /they/ we | like | pizza? |
| Does | she / he/ it | like | chicken? |


Common Mistake: *You like it?*

This may be fine in spoken English, in an informal situation, if you have the proper rising intonation that we use when asking a yes/no question, but not in written English. Simply saying *you like it*, depending on the intonation, may just sound like you're telling someone they like something instead of asking them a question: *Do you like it?*


Exercise 3

Directions: Create a Yes/No question in the present simple tense using the words below. Don't forget to use the correct form: [Do/Does + Subject + Verb + (complement)]

Example: (like pizza/you)

Answer: *Do you like pizza?*

1. (she /know the truth)
2. (have the address/ we)
3. (want coffee/ you)
4. (go to work every day/ your father)
5. (need help/ they)
6. (have internet/ your house)
7. (the food/ taste OK)
8. (need water/ the plants)
9. (smell bad/ I)
10. (New York /have good food)


*Rule 4: To make information questions follow the format:*

*[Wh + Do/Does + Subject + Base Verb + (complement)]*

| Wh | Do/Does | Subject | Base Verb | (complement) |
|----|---------|---------|-----------|--------------|

| What | do | you | eat | for breakfast? |
|------|-----|-----|-------|----------------|
| Where | does | he | live? | |
| How | does | it | work? | |

Exercise 4

Directions: Create an information question in the present simple tense using the words provided. Don't forget to follow the format: [Wh + Do/Does + Subject + Base Verb + (complement)].

Example: (Where/ live/ you)

Answer: *Where do you live?*

1. (What/she/do for work)
2. (Who/ talk to / I)
3. (Where / go on Saturdays/ they)
4. (When/ leave/ you)
5. (Why/ always leave early/ Sara)
6. (How / your sister/ get home)
7. (How often/ they/ brush their teeth)
8. (What time/ get up/ we)
9. (How much/ cost/ that necklace)
10. (How old/ look/ I)

Rule 5: Use the 'be' verb before an adjective or noun. Do NOT use the 'be' verb with any other verbs in the present simple tense.

For example, some English language learners make the following mistakes:

- Incorrect: She *is eats* her breakfast. (Don't combine the 'be' verb with a main verb—eats)
- Correct: She *eats* her breakfast.
- Correct: She *is happy* today. ('happy' is an adjective.)

- Incorrect: I*'m make* a cake every week. (Don't combine the 'be' verb with a main verb—make)
- Correct: I *make* a cake every week.
- Correct: I *am a student*. ('student' is a noun.)
- 

| *Subject* | *Be verb* | *adjective or noun (phrase)* |
|-----------|-----------|------------------------------|
| I | am | happy. |
| He | is | a student. |
| My parents | are | married. |
| We | are | at the zoo. |

Notice in the examples above, when we use the "be" verb in the present simple tense, no other verbs are used.

Rule 6: Do NOT use 'do' or 'does' in questions with the 'be' verb. Only use 'do' or 'does' in the question if there is a main verb (eat, sleep, help, need, etc.)

For example, some students make the following mistakes:

- Incorrect: Do you married?
- Correct: Are you married?

Explanation: "Married" is not a verb; it's an adjective. Since there is no main verb, and since "married" is an adjective, we need to use the 'be' verb.

- Incorrect: Are you live here?
- Correct: Do you live here?
- Correct: Are you here?

Explanation: "live" is a verb, which means that we need to use 'do' in the question. If we take away the verb, then we can use a 'be' verb.

Exercise 5

Directions: Choose the correct answer to fill in the blank.

1. My sister _____ in Sweden.   (live /lives /is live)
2. We _____ to the park every Saturday. (go/ are go/ goes)
3. Those books _____ new. (is/ are/ has)
4. The computer _____. (are not work/ do not work/ does not work)
5. _____ you at home? (Are/ Do/ Does/ Is)
6. _____ Maria have a computer? (Is/ Does/ Do/ Are)
7. _____ they need help? (Does/ Is/ Do/ Are)

*Rule 7: Some information questions in the present simple tense are called "subject questions", which means the questions have a different format. For subject questions, the (Wh) question is the subject. If this is the case, use the following format:*

*[Wh + Verb (s) + complement?]*

Do not use 'do' or 'does in the question and usually the verb will require (s).

| Wh (Subject) | Verb (s) | complement |
|---|---|---|
| Who | lives | here? |
| What time | works | for him? |

| What | makes | them happy? |
|------|-------|-------------|
| What | happens | next? |

After checking your answers, if you feel you need more practice with the present simple tense, there are more exercises in the back of the book which I would recommend doing before continuing onto the next chapter. Otherwise, let's move onto Chapter 6.

Answers to Chapter 5 Exercises:

Answers to Exercise 1:

1. We …..know….. the answer. (know)
2. Mr. Roberts ……….has……. two cars. (have)
3. My computer …….works…… very well. (work)
4. I …….eat….. breakfast every morning at 8:00. (eat)
5. The students ……..need…….more books. (need)
6. This student ………..wants……… another book. (want)
7. Those girls ………….go……….. home at 4:00. (go)
8. My brother ………..goes………. home at 2:00. (go)
9. We ………….do……….our homework at 8:00. (do)
10. My mom always ……….tells…….. me the truth. (tell)

Answers to Exercise 2:

1. Mr. Smith …..doesn't eat…. breakfast. (eat)
2. The students ………don't understand…. their homework. (understand)
3. My sister ………..doesn't like……….her food. (like)
4. My computer ….doesn't work……. (work)
5. The stores ………don't sell……. meat. (sell)
6. My coffee ………….doesn't have……sugar. (have)
7. These tables ………don't cost………..a lot. (cost)
8. That table ……..doesn't cost………. a lot. (cost)
9. They …………..don't smoke……….cigarettes. (smoke)
10. We ………..don't go………. to school on Fridays. (go)

Answers to Exercise 3:

1. (she /know the truth) Does she know the truth?
2. (have the address/ we) Do we have the address?
3. (want coffee/ you) Do you want coffee?
4. (go to work every day/ your father) Does your father go to work every day?
5. (need help/ they) Do they need help?
6. (have internet/ your house) Does your house have internet?
7. (the food/ taste OK) Does the food taste Ok?
8. (need water/ the plants) Do the plants need water?
9. (smell bad/ I) Do I smell bad?
10. (New York /have good food) Does New York have good food?

Answers to Exercise 4:

1. (What/she/do for work) What does she do for work?
2. (Who/ talk to / I) Who do I talk to?
3. (Where / go on Saturdays/ they) Where do they go on Saturdays?
4. (When/ leave/ you) When do you leave?
5. (Why/ always leave early/ Sara) Why does Sara always leave early?
6. (How / your sister/ get home) How does your sister get home?
7. (How often/ they/ brush their teeth) How often do they brush their teeth?
8. (What time/ get up/ we) What time do we get up?
9. (How much/ cost/ that necklace) How much does that necklace cost?
10. (How old/ look/ I) How old do I look?


Answers to Exercise 5:

1. My sister _____ in Sweden.    (live /*lives* /is live)
2. We _____ to the park every Saturday. (*go*/ are go/ goes)
3. Those books _____ new. (is/ *are*/ has)
4. The computer _____. (are not work/ do not work/ *does not work*)
5. _____ you at home? (*Are*/ Do/ Does/ Is)
6. _____ Maria have a computer? (Is/ *Does*/ Do/ Are)
7. _____ they need help? (Does/ Is/ *Do*/ Are)

## Chapter 5 Additional Exercises:

Do the exercises and check your answers before completing the Chapter 3 quiz.

### Exercise 6: Dialogue

Directions: Fill in the blanks with the words from the boxes. One extra word will not be used. Then, if possible, practice the dialogue with a partner.

| are | is | leaves | do | is |
|---|---|---|---|---|
| doesn't | do | are | understand | think |
| does | have | works | is | don't |

A: Excuse me, _____ you Helen?

B: Yes, I am. _____ I know you?

A: No, but you _____ in my English class.

B: Oh, what's your name?

A: My name _____ Adriana. And you?

B: My name is Brian. What do you _____ about our teacher?

A: She _____ know how to teach. She_____ always late. I don't _____ her.

B: Yeah, she _____ class early too.

A: _____ you want to do the homework together? I _____ understand it.

B: Yeah, let's do it. Do you _____ time now?

A: No, I have to go now, but maybe later this afternoon.

B: _____ 3:00 work for you?

A: Yes, that _____ for me. I'll see you then.

B: Ok, see you.

### Exercise 7: Do/Does vs. Is/Am/Are

Directions: For each sentence or question choose one of the words from the box.

| do | does | is | are | am |
|---|---|---|---|---|

1. _____ you have children?

2. _____ you married?
3. What _____ she do for fun?
4. I _____ not want pizza for dinner.
5. _____ I sick?
6. Where _____ you live?
7. She _____ not need more candy.
8. _____ the store open on Sunday?
9. _____ the computer have internet?
10. What time _____ Mr. Ricky get home?
11. They _____ not work after 5pm.


Exercise 8: Find the Mistakes

1. They doesn't want more food.
2. Do you married?
3. Are you eat pizza?
4. She live at home with her parents.
5. The computer is not work very well.


Exercise 9: Discussion questions

1. Do you spend more time inside or outside?
2. Do you need more money?
3. Do you like the food where you live?
4. Do you have children?
5. Do your parents work?
6. Do your shoes smell?
7. Does your family live near you?
8. Does the weather matter to you?
9. Does somebody cook for you?
10. Does your weight go up and down or stay the same?
11. What do you want to do in the future?
12. What do you like to eat for breakfast?
13. Do you use the internet?
14. How many hours do you use the internet per day?
15. What do you use the internet for?
16. What time do you wake up and go to bed?
17. What does "hiccup" mean?
18. Where does your family live?
19. Where do you want to travel?
20. Who do you talk to most?
21. Who do you look like in your family?
22. Who does your laundry?

23. When do you want to get married?
24. What time does the sun set?
25. Why do you want to learn English?
26. Why does money matter?


Chapter 5 Quiz: The Present Simple Tense


Directions: Fill in the blank with the correct form of the verb. Use Present Simple tense.

1. I _____ a new house. (want)
2. My mother _____ pizza. (like)
3. You always _____ your homework. (do)
4. They never _____ on time. (come)
5. My family _____ dinner together. (eat)


Directions: Fill in the blank with the verb. Use the *negative* form of the Present Simple tense.

6. Tina _____ a full time job. (have)
7. I _____ pizza. (like)
8. Simon _____ more work. (want)
9. Most people _____ paid extra money for overtime. (get)
10. A woman _____ to work in my country. (have)


Directions: Use the words below to make questions in the Present Simple Tense.

11. you/ like /pizza
12. when/ the teacher/ come back
13. this restaurant/ have/ good food
14. where/ go to school/ you
15. what/ she/ eat for dinner


Directions: Fill in the blank with the words from the box.

| Do | Does | Is | Am | Are |
|---|---|---|---|---|

16. _____ she speak English?
17. _____ you like your job?
18. _____ you late for class?
19. _____ your mother beautiful?
20. _____ your father eat meat?

21. Why _____ I at the school?
22. Where _____ they work?
23. Where _____ my homework?
24. What _____ "vegetarian" mean?
25. When _____ the concert?

Answers to Additional Exercises Chapter 5

Exercise 6: Dialogue

A: Excuse me, …are… you Helen?

B: Yes, I am. ….Do…. I know you?

A: No, but you …..are…. in my English class.

B: Oh, what's your name?

A: My name ….is……. Adriana. And you?

B: My name is Brian. What do you ……think….. about our teacher?

A: She …….doesn't…… know how to teach. She ….is….always late. I don't …understand…her.

B: Yeah, she ……leaves…..  class early too.

A: …..Do……. you want to do the homework together? I ……don't…… understand it.

B: Yeah, let's do it. Do you ……….have…… time now?

A: No, I have to go now, but maybe later this afternoon.

B: …….Does….. 3:00 work for you?

A: Yes, that ……works….. for me. I'll see you then.

B: Ok, see you.


Exercise 7: Do/Does vs. Am/Is/Are

1. …..Do…. you have children?
2. ……Are…… you married?
3. What …..does…. she do for fun?
4. I ……do…. not want pizza for dinner.
5. ……….Am…… I sick?
6. Where …….do……. you live?
7. She …….does……. not need more candy.
8. …….Does/ Is…… the store open on Sunday? (both answers are possible since "open" is both a verb and a noun)
9. ……….Does……… the computer have internet?
10. What time …….does…….. Mr. Ricky get home?
11. They ………do……… not work after 5pm.


Exercise 8: Find the Mistakes

1. ~~They doesn't want~~ more food. *They don't want* more food. / She doesn't want more food.
2. ~~Do~~ you married? *Are* you married?
3. ~~Are you eat~~ pizza? *Do* you eat pizza?
4. She ~~live~~ at home with her parents. She *lives* at home with her parents.
5. The computer ~~is~~ not work very well. The computer *does* not work very well.


Answers to Chapter 5 Quiz:

1. I want a new house. (want)
2. My mother likes pizza. (like)
3. You always do your homework. (do)
4. They never come on time. (come)
5. My family eats dinner together. (eat)

6. Tina doesn't have a full time job. (have)
7. I don't like pizza. (like)
8. Simon doesn't want more work. (want)
9. Most people don't get paid extra money for overtime. (get)
10. A woman doesn't have to work in my country. (have)

11. you/ like /pizza (Do you like pizza?)
12. when/ the teacher/ come back (When does the teacher come back?)
13. this restaurant/ have/ good food (Does this restaurant have good food?)
14. where/ go to school/ you (Where do you go to school?)
15. what/ she/ eat for dinner (What does she eat for dinner?)

16. Does she speak English?
17. Do you like your job?
18. Are you late for class?
19. Is your mother beautiful?
20. Does your father eat meat?
21. Why am I at the school?
22. Where do they work?
23. Where is my homework?
24. What does "vegetarian" mean?
25. When is the concert?

# Chapter 6: Present Continuous Tense (What are you doing?)

*Rule 1: The present continuous tense uses the following form: [be verb (is/am/are) + verb +ing] and is used to talk about something that is happening right now, at this moment. See the following chart which uses the verb 'to eat'.*

| Subject | be verb | main verb + ing |
|---------|---------|-----------------|
| I | am | eating |
| You | are | eating |
| He | is | eating |
| She | is | eating |
| It | is | eating |
| They | are | eating |
| We | are | eating |

- Example 1: I *am cleaning* my house right now.
- Example 2: He *is doing* his homework.
- Example 3: They *are eating* dinner.

Note that in this tense it is possible to use the "be" verb and a main verb together, but you must add "ing" to the end of the verb.

Spelling Note: verbs that end with a consonant + e (leave, shine, write), drop the final –e and add –ing (leaving, shining, writing)

Exercise 1

Directions: Fill in the blank with the present continuous form.

Example: They _____ outside. (play)

Answer: They *.........are playing............* outside.

1. We _____ to the mountains. (go)
2. I _____ a book. (read)
3. You _____ to music. (listen)
4. My friend Tayna _____ me. (call)
5. My dogs _____. (bark)
6. The sun _____. (shine)

*Rule 2: For the negative form of the present continuous, add not after the 'be' verb and before the main verb.*

| Subject | be (is, am, are) | not | verb-ing | (complement) |
|---|---|---|---|---|
| I | am | not | going | to the party. |
| The kids | are | not | listening | to me. |
| The computer | is | not | working. | |

Exercise 2:

Directions: Fill in the blank with the negative form of the present continuous tense.

Example: We _____ right now. (work)

Answer: We .......*are not working*.... right now.

1. He _____ with us. (go)
2. The TV _____. (work)
3. My parents _____ me alone. (leave)
4. Tina _____ the dishes. (do)
5. My friends and I _____ dinner. (cook)

*Rule 3: To make Yes/No questions in the present continuous form use the following format:*

*[Is/Am/Are + Subject + verb-ing + (complement)]*

| Is/Am/Are | Subject | Verb+ing | (complement) |
|---|---|---|---|
| Are | you | going | to the party? |
| Is | she | dancing? | |
| Am | I | bleeding? | |

Exercise 3

Directions: use the words that are provided to make a Yes/No question in the present continuous tense. Make sure you follow the format: [Am/Is/Are + Subject + verb-ing + (complement)]

Example: (You/listen to me)

Answer: *Are you listening to me?*

1. (he/eat lunch right now)
2. (my mother/call you)
3. (I/ pass the class)
4. (they/play outside)

5. (we/ leave right now)
6. (the car/work well)
7. (it/rain)
8. (the stores/have a sale)
9. (you/ eat healthy)
10. (my friends/ make a cake)


*Rule 4: To make information questions in the present continuous form, use the following format:*

*[Wh + am/is/are + (Subject) + verb-ing + (complement)]*


| Wh | am/is/are | Subject | Verb+ing | (complement) |
|---|---|---|---|---|
| What | are | you | doing? | |
| Where | is | she | going? | |
| How | am | I | doing | in your class? |
| Why | are | they | leaving | so soon? |


Common Mistake: *What we are doing here?*

This type of mistake is noticeable in both spoken and written English. Since this is a question, and not a sentence, we need to put the subject (we) after the *be* verb and before the verb-ing. The correct sentence is: *What are we doing here?*


Exercise 4

Directions: Use the words to make information questions in the present continuous tense.

Example: (Where/you/go)

Answer: *Where are you going?*

1. (Who/he/talk to)
2. (What/we/do)
3. (Where/I/sit)
4. (Why/she/not/come)
5. (How/they/do)
6. (Who/call/me)
7. (What/you/study)
8. (What/Mr. Smith/say)
9. (Where/your friends/take classes)
10. (Why/you/not work)

*Rule 5: Spelling: when adding the –ing, double the final consonant on one syllable verbs that have a [consonant + vowel + consonant] ending (ex: run). Also, when adding –ing to words that end with the letter (e), such as "leave", drop the (e) and add –ing (leaving).*

| Example | Verb | Spelling with –ing | Explanation |
|---------|------|--------------------|-------------|
| 1 | sit | sitting | I need to double the (t) because "sit" is a one syllable word that follows a consonant-vowel-consonant pattern. |
| 2 | eat | eating | I don't need to double the (t) because "eat" is vowel-vowel-consonant. |
| 3 | leave | leaving | Drop the 'e' and add –ing since the verb ends in the letter (e) |

Exercise 5

Directions: add –ing to the following verbs and double the final consonant only if necessary

Example: get

Answer: *getting*

1. sin      _____
2. break    _____
3. cut      _____
4. dig      _____
5. hope     _____

*Rule 6: Don't confuse the Present Simple (chapter 3) with the Present Continuous (what we are learning in this chapter). Use the Present Continuous to talk about something that is happening now, and use the Present Simple (chapter 3) to talk about something that happens always, every day, usually, sometimes, never, or something that is a habit or a fact.*

- Example 1: I *go* to the beach every Saturday. (present simple)
- Example 2: I *am going* to the beach right now. (present continuous)
- Example 3: What *do you do* for work? (present simple)
- Example 4: What *are you doing* now? (present continuous)

Consider the following two sentences:

- I am eating healthy.
- I eat healthy.

The first example (*I am eating healthy*), gives the idea that I'm eating healthy now, these days or this month. The second example (*I eat healthy*) gives the idea that I always eat healthy, every day in general.

Use this chart as a guide:

| Present Simple: [S + verb (s)] [(Wh) + do/does + S + verb?] | Present Continuous [S + is/am/are + verb –ing] [(Wh) + is/am/are + S + verb-ing] |
|---|---|
| Every day, every week, every year | right now |
| always | now |
| sometimes | at this moment |
| never | today |
| usually | this week |
| often | tonight |
| on Saturdays, Sundays, etc. | |

Exercise 6

Directions: Fill in the blank with either the Present Simple or the Present Continuous.

Example 1: I _____ to the movies right now. (go)

Answer 1: I ............*am going*.............. to the movies right now.

Example 2: She _____ to the movies every weekend. (go)

Answer 2: She ........*goes* ..................... to the movies every weekend.

1. They _____ a movie right now. (watch)
2. They _____ a movie every night. (watch)
3. Maria _____ dinner with her family every day. (eat)
4. Maria _____ dinner with her family at the moment. (eat)
5. I always _____ my friend in the summer. (visit)
6. I _____ my friend this week. (visit)
7. What _____ you _____ tonight? (do)
8. What _____ you _____ on Saturdays? (do)

After checking your answers, if you feel you need more practice with the present continuous tense, there are more exercises here, which I would recommend doing before continuing onto the next chapter. Otherwise, let's move onto Chapter 7.

Answers to Exercises Chapter 6

Exercise 1:

1. We ......are going..... to the mountains. (go)
2. I .......am reading..... a book. (read)
3. You ......are listening..... to music. (listen)
4. My friend Tayna ......is calling ......me. (call)
5. My dogs ...........are barking.......... (bark)
6. The sun ..........is shining........ (shine)

Exercise 2:

1. He ............isn't going........ with us. (go)
2. The TV .........isn't working............ (work)
3. My parents .........aren't leaving....... me alone. (leave)
4. Tina ...........isn't doing.......... the dishes. (do)
5. My friends and I .......aren't cooking...... dinner. (cook)

Exercise 3:

1. (he/eat lunch right now) Is he eating lunch right now?
2. (my mother/call you) Is my mother calling you?
3. (I/ pass the class) Am I passing the class?
4. (they/play outside) Are they playing outside?
5. (we/ leave right now) Are we leaving right now?
6. (the car/work well) Is the car working well?
7. (it/rain) Is it raining?
8. (the stores/have a sale) Are the stores having a sale?
9. (you/ eat healthy) Are you eating healthy?
10. (my friends/ make a cake) Are my friends making a cake?

Exercise 4:

1. (Who/he/talk to) Who is he talking to?
2. (What/we/do) What are we doing?
3. (Where/I/sit) Where am I sitting?
4. (Why/she/not/come) Why is she not coming?
5. (How/they/do) How are they doing?
6. (Who/call/me) Who is calling me?
7. (What/you/study) What are you studying?
8. (What/Mr. Smith/say) What is Mr. Smith saying?
9. (Where/your friends/take classes) Where are your friends taking classes?
10. (Why/you/not work) Why are you not working?

Exercise 5:

1. sin      sinning
2. break    breaking
3. cut      cutting
4. dig      digging
5. hope     hoping


Exercise 6:

1. They ....are watching..... a movie right now. (watch)
2. They ..........watch........ a movie every night. (watch)
3. Maria ...............eats..........dinner with her family every day. (eat)
4. Maria ......is eating...... dinner with her family at the moment. (eat)
5. I always ........visit.......my friend in the summer. (visit)
6. I .........am visiting........ my friend this week. (visit)
7. What .....are..... you .........doing..... tonight? (do)
8. What ........do..... you .....do...... on Saturdays? (do)

## Chapter 6 Additional Exercises

### Exercise 7: Dialogue

Directions: Fill in the blanks using the words in the boxes.

| are | take | do | is | helping |
|---|---|---|---|---|
| taking | are | going | is | want |
| doing | I'm | studying | don't | wants |

A: Hey Helen, where _____ you _____?

B: Hi Mike. _____ going to the coffee shop. Do you _____ to come?

A: Sure. What _____ your sister doing? Maybe she _____ to come with us.

B: No, she's _____ at the library right now.

A: Yeah, she's _____ a lot of classes this semester. I always _____the minimum number of classes. I _____ like to be busy.

B: Yeah, same here. What are you _____ later? _____ you want to go see a movie?

A: No, I can't. I'm _____ my roommate move his stuff to another apartment.

B: Ok, maybe later.

A: Is that your friend? What _____ she doing?

B: She's doing yoga.

A: Oh, Ok.

B: Mike? Are we still going to the coffee shop? Why _____ you staring at her?

A: She's so beautiful.


### Exercise 8: Find the mistakes

Directions: Each sentence has a grammar mistake. Identify the error and correct it.

1. Where are you go?
2. She dancing in the street.
3. I'm visiting my grandmother every day.
4. Are you listen to me?
5. The leaves is falling from the tree.
6. What you are doing right now?
7. He's cuting the plants.
8. When are we leaveing?

Exercise 9: Discussion Questions

1. Are you eating healthy these days?
2. Are you gaining weight?
3. Are you dating anyone right now?
4. Are you taking any classes?
5. Are you learning any languages?
6. Is your computer working well?
7. Is your family doing alright?
8. Is this book helping you with your English?
9. Is it raining?
10. Am I speaking too fast?
11. Is the internet working?
12. What are you doing right now?
13. What is your family doing?
14. What are your friends doing?
15. What goals are you working on?
16. Who are you talking to?
17. Who is your best friend dating?
18. Where are you going?
19. Where is the dog hiding?
20. Why are you learning English?
21. Why is it raining so hard?

Chapter 6 Quiz

Directions: Fill in the blank with the Present Continuous tense using the verb provided. If you see "not", put the verb in the negative form of the tense.

1. I _____ to the teacher right now. (listen)
2. She _____ a book at the moment. (read)
3. They _____ sentences today. (not, write)
4. Simon _____ his car right now.
5. You _____ your money in the bank. (not, put)

Directions: Make questions in the Present Continuous tense using the following words.

6. (pass the class/ I)
7. (she/ read a book)
8. (eat dinner/ he)
9. (what /you/ do)
10. (why/ he/ wait in line)

Directions: Use the verb at the end of the sentence to fill in the blank with either the Present Continuous tense or the Present Simple tense.

11. What _____ you _____ on the weekends? (do)
12. My sister can't come. She _____ now. (study)
13. My students this semester_____ very quickly. (learn)
14. Mr. Smith _____ with someone at the moment. (speak)
15. Timothy _____ eggs every morning for breakfast. (eat)

Answers to Additional Exercises Chapter 6:

Exercise 7: Dialogue

A: Hey Helen, where …are…. you ….going…?

B: Hi Mike. ….I'm…… going to the coffee shop. Do you ……want….. to come?

A: Sure. What …..is…… your sister doing? Maybe she ……wants…. to come with us.

B: No, she's …..studying….. at the library right now.

A: Yeah, she's …….taking…… a lot of classes this semester. I always …..take…..the minimum number of classes. I …….don't…… like to be busy.

B: Yeah, same here. What are you ……..doing…… later? ……….Do…… you want to go see a movie?

A: No, I can't. I'm ……..helping….. my roommate move his stuff to another apartment.

B: Ok, maybe later.

A: Is that your friend? What …..is…….. she doing?

B: She's doing yoga.

A: Oh, Ok.

B: Mike? Are we still going to the coffee shop? Why ……..are…….you staring at her?

A: She's so beautiful.


Exercise 8: Find the Mistakes

1. Where are you ~~go?~~ Where are you *going*?
2. ~~She dancing~~ in the street. She *is dancing* in the street.
3. ~~I'm visiting~~ my grandmother every day. *I visit* my grandmother every day.
4. ~~Are you listen~~ to me? *Are you listening* to me?
5. ~~The leaves is~~ falling from the tree. *The leaves are* falling from the tree.
6. What ~~you are~~ doing right now? What *are you* doing right now?
7. He's ~~cuting~~ the plants. He's *cutting* the plants.
8. When are we ~~leaveing~~? When are we *leaving*?


Answers to Chapter 6 Quiz:

1. I ………am listening……. to the teacher right now. (listen)
2. She ………….is reading…….. a book at the moment. (read)
3. They ……….are not writing………. sentences today. (not, write)
4. Simon ……….is fixing…….. his car right now. (fix)

5. You …………are not putting……. your money in the bank. (not, put)

6.  (pass the class/ I) Am I passing the class?
7. (she/ read a book) Is she reading a book?
8. (eat dinner/ he) Is he eating dinner?
9. (what /you/ do) What are you doing?
10. (why/ he/ wait in line) Why is he waiting in line?

11. What ……do……. you ……….do……….. on the weekends? (do)
12. My sister can't come. She ………..is studying…….. now. (study)
13. My students this semester ………..are learning……very quickly. (learn)
14. Mr. Smith ……..is speaking…… with someone at the moment. (speak)
15. Timothy ………..eats……..eggs every morning for breakfast. (eat)

# Chapter 7: The Future Simple Tense (What are you going to do?)

*Rule 1a: There are two grammar structures used to talk about the future.*

1.  *[Subject + am/is/are + going to + base verb]*

| Subject | am/is/are | going to | base verb |
|---------|-----------|----------|-----------|
| I | am | going to | sleep |
| He | is | going to | dance |
| She | is | going to | eat |
| It | is | going to | work |
| You | are | going to | see |
| They | are | going to | enjoy it |
| We | are | going to | have a coffee |

2.  *[Subject + will + base verb]*

| Subject | will | base verb |
|---------|------|-----------|
| I | will | sleep |
| He | will | dance |
| She | will | eat |
| It | will | work |
| You | will | see |
| They | will | enjoy it |
| We | will | have a coffee |

Contractions:

| I will | I'll |
|--------|------|
| He will | He'll |
| She will | She'll |
| It will | It'll |
| You will | You'll |
| They will | They'll |
| We will | We'll |

*Rule 1b: We generally use the 'be going to' form to talk about definite goals, future events and future plans, while we generally use 'will' to talk about spontaneous decisions made at the moment of speaking.*

- Example 1: This weekend *I'm going to have* a party at my house. (This is a plan)
- Example 2: Next month my sister *is going to have* her baby. (This is a future event)

- Example 3: This year *I'm going to save* more money. (This is a future goal)
- Example 4: The phone is ringing. *I'll get* it! (This is a spontaneous decision)
- Example 5: A: There's a party tonight at Marie's house. B: Oh really? Maybe *I'll go*. (This is a decision at the moment of speaking)
- Example 6: A: I need a volunteer. B: *I'll do* it! (This is a spontaneous decision)

Exercise 1

Directions: Decide if you should use 'be going to' or 'will' in the following sentences and fill in the blanks with the correct Future Simple form.

Example: Tonight I _____ at the new restaurant with Susan. Do you want to come? (eat)

Answer: Tonight I ..........*am going to eat*..........................at the new restaurant with Susan. Do you want to come?

1. A: Somebody is knocking on the door. B: I _____ it. (get)
2. This year I _____ $500. (save)
3. My sister _____ you tonight. (call)
4. Look, that woman needs help. I _____ her. (help)
5. The news said that tomorrow it _____. (rain)

*Rule 2: To make a negative statement using the Future Simple forms, use the following formulas.*

1. *[Subject + is/am/are + not +going to + verb]*

| Subject | is/are/am | not | going to | verb |
|---|---|---|---|---|
| I | am | not | going to | cook |
| He /She /It | is | not | going to | cook |
| They /We/ You | are | not | going to | cook |

2. *[Subject + will + not + verb]*

| Subject | will | not | verb |
|---|---|---|---|
| I | will | not | do it |
| He | will | not | do it |
| They | will | not | do it |

Note: The contraction of "will not" = *won't*

- o Example: I won't do it.
- o Example: We won't do it.

Common Mistake: *I'm gonna do it.*

This is fine most of the time in spoken English, but never in formal or semi-formal written English. The word *'gonna'* should never be written, only spoken. Write out the full form: *I'm going to do it.*

Exercise 2: Fill in the blank with the negative form of the Future Simple tense. Use either form.

1. I _____ help you. You need to find someone else.
2. They _____ be there. They left the country.
3. My sister _____ understand. You shouldn't tell her.
4. The door _____ open. We need to call someone.
5. We _____ eat all your food. Relax.

*Rule 3: To make a Yes/No questions in the Future Simple tense, use the following forms.*

1. *[Is/Am/Are + Subject + going to + verb?]*

| Is / Am/ Are | Subject | going to | Verb |
|---|---|---|---|
| Am | I | going to | like it? |
| Is | he/she/it | going to | cook? |
| Are | you/they/we | going to | help? |

2. *[Will + Subject + verb]*

| Will | Subject | verb |
|---|---|---|
| Will | I | have time? |
| Will | he | do it? |
| Will | they | cook dinner? |

Exercise 3

Directions: Use the words below to make Yes/No questions in the Future Simple tense. Use either of the two tenses or both. There will be two possible answers.

Example: (we/eat dinner)

| Answer 1 | Answer 2 |
|---|---|
| Are we going to eat dinner? | Will we eat dinner? |

Answer: *Are we going to eat dinner?* **OR** *Will we eat dinner?*

1. (he/listen)

2. (you/wash my clothes)
3. (I /be in trouble)
4. (Maria/drive to work)
5. (They/watch a movie)

*Rule 4: To make an information question in the Future Simple tense, use the following formulas.*

1. *[Wh + is/am/are + S + going to + verb?]*

| (Wh) word | is/am/are | Subject | going to | verb |
|-----------|-----------|---------|----------|------|
| What | are | you /they/ we | going to | do? |
| Who | is | he/ she/ it | going to | call? |
| Where | am | I | going to | study? |

2. *[Wh + will + S + verb]*

| (Wh) word | will | Subject | verb |
|-----------|------|---------|------|
| When | will | he | return? |
| How | will | you | get to school? |
| What | will | they | bring? |

Exercise 4

Directions: Use the words below to make information questions using the Future Simple tense. There are two possible answers for each number.

Example: (Where/you/watch the game)

| Answer 1 | Answer 2 |
|----------|----------|
| Where are you going to watch the game? | Where will you watch the game? |

1. (What/you/do after school)
2. (Where/she/go to college)
3. (Who/we/tell)
4. (When/they/eat lunch)
5. (How/my sister/ find me)

*Rule 5: The Present Continuous tense can also be used to talk about the future.*

Even though in Chapter 3, we learned that the present continuous (I am doing) is used to talk about what is happening right now, it can also be used to talk about the future instead of the 'be going to' form. Generally, the present continuous is used for future meaning when it is based on a timetable or a schedule. Check out the following examples.

| Present Continuous (be + verb + ing) | Future Simple (be + going to + verb) |
|---|---|
| Tonight *I'm having* a party. | Tonight *I'm going to have* a party. |
| They *are arriving* at 8:00 tomorrow. | They *are going to arrive* at 8:00 tomorrow. |
| What time *are you going* to the doctor? | What time *are you going to go* to the doctor? |
| Next Tuesday, *I'm leaving* school early. | Next Tuesday, *I'm going to leave* school early. |

The sentences above all have the same meaning.


After checking your answers, if you feel you need more practice with the future simple, go to Chapter 7 additional exercises, which I would recommend doing before continuing onto the next chapter. Otherwise, let's move onto Chapter 8.

## Answers to Chapter 7 Exercises

Exercise 1:

1. A: Somebody is knocking on the door. B: I ........will get....... it. (get)
2. This year I ..........am going to save........ $500. (save)
3. My sister ................is going to call...... you tonight. (call)
4. Look, that woman needs help. I ..........will help.........her. (help)
5. The news said that tomorrow it .........is going to rain........... (rain)

Exercise 2:

1. I ......will not/ won't / am not going to..... help you. You need to find someone else.
2. They ..........will not/ won't / are not going to ......be there. They left the country.
3. My sister ..........will not/ won't/ is not going to ..... understand. You shouldn't tell her.
4. The door ..........will not/ won't/ is not going to.... open. We need to call someone.
5. We ..........will not/ won't/ are not going to ....... eat all your food. Relax.

Exercise 3:

1. (he/listen) Is he going to listen? / Will he listen?
2. (you/wash my clothes) Are you going to wash my clothes? / Will you wash my clothes?
3. (I /be in trouble) Am I going to be in trouble? / Will I be in trouble?
4. (Maria/drive to work) Is Maria going to drive to work? / Will Maria drive to work?
5. (They/watch a movie) Are they going to watch a movie? / Will they watch a movie?

Exercise 4:

1. (What/you/do after school) What are you going to do after school? / What will you do after school?
2. (Where/she/go to college) Where is she going to go to college? / Where will she go to college?
3. (Who/we/tell) Who are we going to tell? / Who will we tell?
4. (When/they/eat lunch) When are they going to eat their lunch? /When will they eat their lunch?
5. (How/my sister/ find me) How is my sister going to find me? / How will my sister find me?

Exercise 5: Dialogue

Directions: Fill in the blanks with the words from the box.

| be | is playing | bring | does | stay |
|---|---|---|---|---|
| going to | lives | I'll | is having | will call |
| She'll | is going to be | am going | let | won't |

A: Mike, it's Friday. What are you _____ do tonight?

B: Not sure. Maybe _____ go to that party at Sara's house. What about you?

A: I'm probably going to _____ at home and do nothing, but I'm not sure. I'll _____you know.

B: Don't forget. On Saturday there _____ a concert in the park at 4:00. My band _____.

A: I _____forget. Don't worry. I _____ to bring my sister with me. _____ enjoy it.

B: I hope so. She'll probably _____ her books and just study the whole time.

A: No, don't worry. I won't let her.

B: It'll _____ fun.

A: Oh, and on Sunday, my friend Marie _____ a BBQ at her house if you want to come.

B: Marie? Where _____ she live?

A: She _____ a few streets down from me.

B: Ok cool. I'll just go to your house first and then we can walk over together.

A: Sounds like a plan. I_____ you later.

B: See ya!


Exercise 6: Find the Mistakes

Directions: There is one sentence that is correct and all the others have errors. Find the mistakes and correct the sentence.

1. When are you going to leaving?
2. I will to give you the information later.
3. What are you do here?
4. She going to miss you.
5. They want talk to me.
6. I am will be there.

7. My favorite movie is playing at 5:00 tomorrow.
8. We going to be here at the house.


Exercise 7: Discussion Questions

Directions: Write your answers to the questions or find someone to discuss the questions with.

1. Are you going to get married or are you going to stay single forever?
2. How many children are you going to have?
3. Are you going to study more in the future?
4. What are you going to study?
5. Where are you going to live in the future?
6. Are you going to stay in the same place for the rest of your life?
7. Is somebody in your family going to retire soon?
8. How old are you going to be when you retire?
9. When are you going to speak English perfectly?
10. Who are you going to spend time with tonight?
11. Who are you going to see tomorrow?
12. Where are you going to travel in the future?
13. What events are going to happen in the future?
14. Is it going to rain tomorrow?
15. What are you going to do tomorrow, this weekend?
16. What is going to happen with the environment in the future?
17. What inventions are humans going to invent in the future?
18. How are cars going to change in the future?
19. How are families going to change in the future?
20. How will society change in the future?


Chapter 7 Quiz


Directions: Fill in the blank with the Future Simple tense. Use the 'be going to' form. Use the verbs provided and if there is "not" with the verb, use the negative form.

1. My sister _____ to New York next week. (move)
2. The computers _____ anymore. (not, work)
3. I _____ my job next Tuesday. (quit)
4. The cat _____ inside anymore. (not, stay)
5. My parents _____ soon. (retire)


Directions: Fill in the blank with the Future Simple tense. Use the "will" form. Use the verbs provided and if you see a word "not" with the verb, use the negative form.

6. The door _____ . (not open)
7. Marie _____ enough time to do her homework. (not have)
8. If you take care of your clothes, they _____ a long time. (last)
9. I _____ a cake to the party. (bring)
10. We _____ if somebody calls. (answer)


Directions: Use the words below to make questions in the Future Simple tense. Use the 'be going to' form.

11. (you/ dance/ at the party)
12. (When/ she/ learn English)
13. (How/ they/ get to school)
14. (What/ we/ do / tonight)
15. (Who /I /call)


Directions: Use the words below to make questions in the Future Simple tense. Use the "will" form.

16. (you/ dance/ at the party)
17. (When/ she/ learn English)
18. (How/ they/ get to school)
19. (What/ we/ do / tonight)
20. (Who /I /call)

Exercise 5: Dialogue

A: Mike, it's Friday. What are you .......going to......... do tonight?

B: Not sure. Maybe ......I'll.... go to that party at Sara's house. What about you?

A: I'm probably going to .....stay..... at home and do nothing, but I'm not sure. I'll .....let....you know.

B: Don't forget. On Saturday there ......is going to be..... a concert in the park at 4:00. My band .....is playing......

A: I ......won't.....forget. Don't worry. I ....am going.....to bring my sister with me. .....She'll..... enjoy it.

B: I hope so. She'll probably ....bring..... her books and just study the whole time.

A: No, don't worry. I won't let her.

B: It'll ........be.......fun.

A: Oh, and on Sunday, my friend Marie ..........is having...... a BBQ at her house if you want to come.

B: Marie? Where .....does..... she live?

A: She ........lives........ a few streets down from me.

B: Ok cool. I'll just go to your house first and then we can walk over together.

A: Sounds like a plan. I......will call... you later.

B: See ya!


Exercise 6: Find the Mistakes

1. When are you going to leaving? When are you going *to leave*?
2. I will to give you the information later. I *will give* you the information later.
3. What are you do here? What are you *doing* here?
4. She going to miss you. *She is going* to miss you.
5. They want talk to me. They *won't* talk to me.
6. I am will be there. I *will be* there. / I *am going to be* there.
7. My favorite movie is playing at 5:00 tomorrow. Correct
8. We going to be here at the house. *We are going* to be here at the house.


Answers to Chapter 7 Quiz:

1. My sister .....is going to move..... to New York next week. (move)
2. The computers .....are not going to work.... anymore. (not, work)
3. I ..........am going to quit.... my job next Tuesday. (quit)

4. The cat ........is not going to stay....... inside anymore. (not, stay)
5. My parents .........are going to retire..... soon. (retire)

6. The door .......will not /won't open....... (not open)
7. Marie .......will not/ won't have... enough time to do her homework. (not have)
8. If you take care of your clothes, they .....will last ..... a long time. (last)
9. I ........will bring......a cake to the party. (bring)
10. We ..........will answer........ if somebody calls. (answer)

11. (you/ dance/ at the party) Are you going to dance at the party?
12. (When/ she/ learn English) When is she going to learn English?
13. (How/ they/ get to school) How are they going to get to school?
14. (What/ we/ do / tonight) What are we going to do tonight?
15. (Who /I /call) Who am I going to call?

16. (you/ dance/ at the party) Will you dance at the party?
17. (When/ she/ learn English) When will she learn English?
18. (How/ they/ get to school) How will they get to school?
19. (What/ we/ do / tonight) What will we do tonight?
20. (Who /I /call) Who will I call?

# Chapter 8: The Past Simple Tense (What did you do?)

There are three main tenses used to talk about the past, but we are going to focus on the Past Simple, the most common form of the past tense.

| Tense | Example |
|---|---|
| Past Simple | I *helped* her yesterday. |
| Past Continuous | I *was helping* her when it started to rain. |
| Past Perfect | I *had helped* her before I went home. |

*Rule 1: To use the Past Simple tense, add the letters (-ed) to most verbs (verb +ed). The subject does not change the form of the verb. [Subject + verb-ed + complement]*

| Base Verb | Past simple | Example Sentence |
|---|---|---|
| help | helped | I *helped* her yesterday. |
| need | needed | I *needed* help. |
| jump | jumped | I *jumped* from an airplane last year. |
| look | looked | I *looked* at the clock. |

*Rule 1b: For verbs that end in the letter (e), simply add the letter (d)*

| Verb | Past Simple form |
|---|---|
| save | saved |
| bribe | bribed |
| care | cared |

*Rule 1c: For verbs that end in a consonant + y, drop the y and add (-ied). However, for verbs that end in a vowel + y, keep the y and just add –ed.*

| verb | verb ending | Past Simple form |
|---|---|---|
| cry | consonant + y (ry) | cried |
| play | vowel + y (ay) | played |
| study | consonant + y (dy) | studied |

Exercise 1

Directions: Fill in the blank with the Past Simple tense using the verb provided

Example: I _____ $100 last week. (save)

Answer: I ............saved..................... $100 last week.

1. My sister _____ her last name when she got married. (change)
2. The children _____ TV for two hours last night. (watch)
3. We _____ outside in the rain yesterday. (play)
4. You _____ up the kids from school late. (pick)
5. I _____ three times yesterday. (surf)

*Rule 2: Some verbs in English are irregular, meaning they don't follow the rules, so instead of adding –ed to the verb, or following the spelling rules listed above, you need to memorize the past form of the verb.*

The following chart lists the 25 most common irregular verbs.

| Base Verb | Past Simple form |
| --- | --- |
| say | said |
| make | made |
| go | went |
| take | took |
| come | came |
| see | saw |
| know | knew |
| get | got |
| give | gave |
| find | found |
| think | thought |
| tell | told |
| become | became |
| meet | met |
| leave | left |
| feel | felt |
| put | put |
| bring | brought |
| begin | began |
| keep | kept |
| hold | held |
| write | wrote |
| stand | stood |
| hear | heard |
| let | let |

| | |
|---|---|
| read | read |
| drive | drove |

Exercise 2:

Directions: Fill in the blank with the correct form of the Past Simple. Use the chart above to help you with the irregular verbs.

1. I _____ outside in the rain for two hours. (stand)
2. Mr. Ricky _____ not to eat that. (say)
3. We _____ to the party last night but we didn't see you. (come)
4. The child _____ that her mother had died. (know)
5. Yesterday Maria _____ a cake for you. (make)
6. You _____ to the wrong store. (go)
7. I _____ sick last week. (feel)

*Rule 3: For negative sentences in the Past Simple tense, place "did not" (didn't) before the verb, and do not add –ed to the verb. This is the following formula for Past Simple tense:*

*[Subject + did not + base verb + (complement)]*

Remember, base verb = do not change the form of the verb; do not put –ed or change it to the irregular form. By putting "did" in the sentence, we are indicating the past tense, so we do not need to put the past tense twice in the sentence.

| Subject | did not (didn't) | base verb | (complement) |
|---|---|---|---|
| I | didn't | see | you. |
| You | didn't | come | to my party. |
| He | didn't | know. | |
| She | didn't | need | your help. |
| It | didn't | work. | |
| They | didn't | answer | the phone. |
| We | didn't | make | an appointment. |

Common Mistake: *We didn't made an appointment.*

*Didn't* already indicates past tense. Therefore, we do not need to put the verb in the past tense. When using the negative form of the Past Simple (didn't), use the base verb after: *We didn't* make an appointment.

Exercise 3

Directions: Fill in the blank with the negative form of the Past Simple.

1. Maria _____ her keys. (find)
2. Mr. and Mrs. Smith _____ to the party. (come)
3. I _____ that you have children. (know)
4. You _____ to help. (need)
5. The dogs _____ their medicine. (take)

*Rule 4: To create a Yes/No question in the Past Simple tense, use the following formula.*

*[Did + Subject + base verb + (complement)?]*

| Did | Subject | base verb | (complement) |
|-----|---------|-----------|--------------|
| Did | you | go | to the party? |
| Did | she | meet | anybody? |
| Did | the children | enjoy | their day? |
| Did | my brothers | leave | already? |
| Did | Mr. Smith | need | something? |

Common Mistake: *Did you went to my house?*

Just as the previous mistake, "Did" already represents the past, so we don't need to put the main verb (go) in the past tense. Use the base form of the verb in questions with "did" (*Did you go to my house?*).

Exercise 4

Directions: Use the words provided to create Yes/No questions in the Past Simple tense

1. (you/ have fun yesterday)
2. (he/say goodbye)
3. (your cat/ disappear)
4. (Marie/ buy the book)
5. (they /see that movie)

*Rule 5: To create an information question in the Past Simple tense, use the following formula.*

*[Wh + did + Subject + verb + (complement)?]*

| Wh | did | subject | verb | (complement) |
|----|-----|---------|------|--------------|
| Why | did | you | leave | so early? |

| Who | did | they | visit | in the hospital? |
|---|---|---|---|---|
| What | did | you | do | last night? |
| Where | did | Mr. Smith | go? | |
| When | did | I | call | you? |

Exercise 5

Directions: Use the words provided to create information questions in the Past Simple tense

1. (Where/you/go/last night)
2. (When/she /leave)
3. (Who/ they/see/yesterday)
4. (What/we/do/ last summer)
5. (Why/Michael/call me)
6. (How/you/meet her)

Note: As with most of the tenses there are "subject questions", in which the question word (Who, What) is the subject, so there is a different form for these questions. See the examples in the chart.

[Wh + past form of verb + (complement)]

| Wh word (Subject) | Verb (past simple form) | complement |
|---|---|---|
| Who | saw | this? |
| What | happened? | |
| Who | lived | here? |

Rule 6: To use the 'be' verb in the Past Simple, use "was" or "were". Use the following charts as a guide. Don't use the 'be' verb (was, were) with any other main verb in the Past Simple tense.

| Subject | Be Verb (Past Simple) |
|---|---|
| I /he/ she/ it | was |
| You/ they/ we | were |

| Be Verb (Past Simple) | Examples | Form |
|---|---|---|
| Affirmative | I was a student at this school. You *were* here yesterday. They *were* angry. | [Subject + was/were + adj. or noun (phrase)] |
| Negative | I *was not* a student at this school. | [Subject + was/were + not + adj. or noun |

|  | You *were not* with me.<br>She *was not* very happy. | (phrase)] |
| Yes/No Question | *Were* you upset?<br>*Was* Marie sick last week?<br>*Were* my sisters there? | [Was/Were + Subject + adj. or noun (phrase)] |
| Information Question | When *were* you at the hospital?<br>Why was she *late*?<br>How *was* the movie? | [Wh + was/were + Subject + adj. or noun (phrase)] |

## Exercise 6

Directions: Fill in the blanks with either "was" or "were"

1. Mr. Caputo _____ late every day last week.
2. My pants _____ wet from the rain.
3. I _____ never friends with her.
4. You _____ at the party last night.
5. We _____ not good friends.

## Exercise 7

Directions: Create questions using the "be" verb in the Past Simple tense with the words below.

1. (When/you/born)
2. (Why /she/ late)
3. (I /asleep)
4. (What /they/ upset about)
5. (Where /we/ yesterday at 8:00)

Answers to Exercises Chapter 8

Exercise 1:

1. My sister ......changed......her last name when she got married. (change)
2. The children .......watched....... TV for two hours last night. (watch)
3. We .............played......... outside in the rain yesterday. (play)
4. You ..........picked........ up the kids from school late. (pick)
5. I .........surfed..........three times yesterday. (surf)

Exercise 2:

1. I .........stood.......... outside in the rain for two hours. (stand)
2. Mr. Ricky .............said............ not to eat that. (say)
3. We ...........came......... to the party last night but we didn't see you. (come)
4. The child ............knew........ that her mother had died. (know)
5. Yesterday Maria .............made........ a cake for you. (make)
6. You .............went........ to the wrong store. (go)
7. I ............felt........... sick last week. (feel)

Exercise 3:

1. Maria .......didn't find....... her keys. (find)
2. Mr. and Mrs. Smith ............didn't come.......... to the party. (come)
3. I ........didn't know........that you have children. (know)
4. You ............didn't need............to help. (need)
5. The dogs ...........didn't take....... their medicine. (take)

Exercise 4:

1. (you/ have fun yesterday) Did you have fun yesterday?
2. (he/say goodbye) Did he say goodbye?
3. (your cat/ disappear) Did your cat disappear?
4. (Marie/ buy the book) Did Marie buy the book?
5. (they /see that movie) Did they see that movie?

Exercise 5:

1. (Where/you/go/last night) Where did you go last night?
2. (When/she /leave) When did she leave?
3. (Who/ they/see/yesterday) Who did they see yesterday?

4. (What/we/do/ last summer) What did we do last summer?
5. (Why/Michael/call me) Why did Michael call me?
6. (How/you/meet her) How did you meet her?


Exercise 6:

1. Mr. Caputo .........was......... late every day last week.
2. My pants .......were....... wet from the rain.
3. I .......was......... never friends with her.
4. You ..........were........ at the party last night.
5. We ..........were........ not good friends.


Exercise 7

1. (When/you/born) When were you born?
2. (Why /she/ late) Why was she late?
3. (I /asleep) Was I asleep?
4. (What /they/ upset about) What were they upset about?
5. (Where /we/ yesterday at 8:00) Where were we yesterday at 8:00?

Chapter 8 Additional Exercises

Exercise 8: More Practice with Irregular Verbs

Directions: Fill in the blanks with the correct form of the verb in the Past Simple. For a more complete list of irregular verbs, see Appendix A.

| Verb | Past Simple Form |
|---|---|
| 1. take | |
| 2. have | |
| 3. get | |
| 4. see | |
| 5. make | |
| 6. eat | |
| 7. write | |
| 8. think | |
| 9. come | |
| 10. leave | |
| 11. go | |
| 12. drive | |
| 13. find | |
| 14. buy | |
| 15. fall | |
| 16. know | |
| 17. give | |
| 18. break | |
| 19. feel | |
| 20. meet | |
| 21. do | |
| 22. read | |
| 23. say | |
| 24. tell | |
| 25. understand | |

Exercise 9: Dialogue

Directions: Fill in the blank with the correct words from the box.

| did | was | don't | lost | saw |
|---|---|---|---|---|
| did | put | invite | see | do |
| was | called | were | stayed | didn't |

A: Helen, where _____ you yesterday?

B: Hey Mike. I _____ at the movies with my sister.

A: Oh really? What movie _____ you _____?

B: We _____ Mr. and Mrs. Smith. It _____ a great movie.

A: Why didn't you _____ me?

B: I _____ you three times, but you _____ answer.

A: Yeah, I _____ my phone. I can't find it anywhere.

B: Oh no! Where _____ you _____ it last?

A: I _____ remember. I think I have to buy a new one.

B: What did you _____ yesterday?

A: I _____at home because I couldn't call anyone.

B: Yeah, you need to get a new phone.


Exercise 10: Find the Mistakes

Directions: Each sentence has a mistake. Identify the error and correct the sentence.

1. Who you saw last night at the party?
2. I leaved the house at 8:00 this morning.
3. Do you get the book yesterday?
4. Was you at the bank this morning?
5. I called you last night, but you didn't answered.
6. Why you were not at work today?
7. I was not eat because I was not hungry.


Exercise 11: Discussion Questions in the Past Simple

1. Did you have a good day yesterday?
2. Did you eat lunch yet?
3. Did your parents reward you for good grades as a child?
4. Were you a good child?
5. Were your parents strict?
6. Did you share a room?
7. Did your family always eat meals together when you were a child?
8. Were there any pets in your family?
9. Was the weather good yesterday?
10. Was the food good last night?
11. What was your favorite movie as a child?
12. Who was your favorite actor as a child?

13. Where were you born?
14. What was good about yesterday?
15. Who were your friends when you were a child?
16. As a child, what? did you want to be when you grew up?
17. Where did you travel to last year?
18. When did you start to learn English?
19. How was your breakfast?
20. What was the last movie you saw? How was it?
21. Where did you go yesterday?


Chapter 8 Quiz


Directions: Fill in the blank with the Past Simple form of the verb in parentheses. Some verbs may be irregular, and some ask for the negative form.

1. Yesterday Sara _____ to the concert. (go)
2. Last week I _____ her at the mall. (see)
3. My cousins _____ at the meeting. (be)
4. You _____ extra clothes. I have enough here. (not need)
5. My brothers and I _____ home. (not be)
6. Mike _____ for two hours yesterday. (surf)
7. Last year I _____ in school. Now I'm working. (be)
8. We _____ that you were in the hospital. (not know)
9. My computer _____ working this morning. (stop)
10. The students _____ class early. (leave)

Directions: Use the words below to make questions in the Past Simple tense.

11. (Where/ you/ be/ yesterday)
12. (you/ have fun/ yesterday)
13. (I/ late/ be/ last week)
14. (he/ eat dinner)
15. (they/ be/ at the movies with you)
16. (When / they/ come home)
17. (What/ the answer/ be)
18. (Why/ you/ do that)
19. (Who/ you with/ be)
20. (How/ get here/ she)

Exercise 8: Irregular Verbs

| Verb | Past Simple Form |
|---|---|
| 1. take | took |
| 2. have | had |
| 3. get | got |
| 4. see | saw |
| 5. make | made |
| 6. eat | ate |
| 7. write | wrote |
| 8. think | thought |
| 9. come | came |
| 10. leave | left |
| 11. go | went |
| 12. drive | drove |
| 13. find | found |
| 14. buy | bought |
| 15. fall | fell |
| 16. know | knew |
| 17. give | gave |
| 18. break | broke |
| 19. feel | felt |
| 20. meet | met |
| 21. do | did |
| 22. read | read |
| 23. say | said |
| 24. tell | told |
| 25. understand | understood |

Exercise 9: Dialogue

A: Helen, where ….were…. you yesterday?

B: Hey Mike. I …..was……. at the movies with my sister.

A: Oh really? What movie …….did…… you ………see…….?

B: We …….saw……..Mr. and Mrs. Smith. It ……..was……. a great movie.

A: Why didn't you ………invite…… me?

B: I …………called……… you three times, but you ………didn't…… answer.

A: Yeah, I ……..lost……. my phone. I can't find it anywhere.

B: Oh no! Where ........did....... you ........put........ it last?

A: I .........don't....... remember. I think I have to buy a new one.

B: What did you .........do.........yesterday?

A: I ............stayed.........at home because I couldn't call anyone.

B: Yeah, you need to get a new phone.


## Exercise 10: Find the Mistakes

1. Who ~~you saw~~ last night at the party? Who *did you see* last night at the party?
2. I ~~leaved~~ the house at 8:00 this morning. I *left* the house at 8:00 this morning.
3. ~~Do~~ you get the book yesterday? *Did* you get the book yesterday?
4. ~~Was~~ you at the bank this morning? *Were you* at the bank this morning?
5. I called you last night, but you didn't ~~answered~~. I called you last night, but you *didn't answer.*
6. Why ~~you were~~ not at work today? Why *were you* not at work today?
7. I ~~was not eat~~ because I was not hungry. I *didn't eat* because I was not hungry.


## Chapter 8 Quiz:

1. Yesterday Sara ......went..... to the concert. (go)
2. Last week I ............saw........ her at the mall. (see)
3. My cousins ...........were......... at the meeting. (be)
4. You ...........didn't need...... extra clothes. I have enough here. (not need)
5. My brothers and I ...........were not.......... home. (not be)
6. Mike .........surfed........... for two hours yesterday. (surf)
7. Last year I ............was........... in school. Now I'm working. (be)
8. We .................didn't know......... that you were in the hospital. (not know)
9. My computer .............stopped...... working this morning. (stop)
10. The students .............left........... class early. (leave)

11. (Where/ you/ be/ yesterday) Where were you yesterday?
12. (you/ have fun/ yesterday) Did you have fun yesterday?
13. (I/ late/ be/ last week) Was I late last week?
14. (he/ eat dinner) Did he eat dinner?
15. (they/ be/ at the movies with you) Were they at the movies with you?
16. (When / they/ come home) When did they come home?
17. (What/ the answer/ be) What was the answer?
18. (Why/ you/ do that) Why did you do that?
19. (Who/ you with/ be) Who were you with?
20. (How/ get here/ she) How did she get here?

# Appendix A: More Irregular Verbs

| Verb (base form) | Past Simple |
|---|---|
| be | was, were |
| beat | beat |
| become | became |
| begin | began |
| bend | bent |
| bid | bid |
| bite | bit |
| blow | blew |
| break | broke |
| bring | brought |
| build | built |
| burn | burnt |
| buy | bought |
| catch | caught |
| choose | chose |
| come | came |
| cost | cost |
| cut | cut |
| dig | dug |
| do | did |
| draw | drew |
| drive | drove |
| drink | drank |
| eat | ate |
| fall | fell |
| feel | felt |
| fight | fought |
| find | found |
| fly | flew |
| forget | forgot |
| forgive | forgave |
| freeze | froze |
| get | got |
| give | gave |
| go | went |
| grow | grew |
| hang | hung |
| have | had |
| hear | heard |
| hide | hid |
| hit | hit |
| hold | held |

| | |
|---|---|
| hurt | hurt |
| keep | kept |
| know | knew |
| lead | led |
| leave | left |
| lend | lent |
| let | let |
| lose | lost |
| make | made |
| mean | meant |
| meet | met |
| pay | paid |
| put | put |
| read | read |
| ride | rode |
| ring | rang |
| run | ran |
| say | said |
| see | saw |
| sell | sold |
| send | sent |
| shut | shut |
| sing | sang |
| sit | sat |
| sleep | slept |
| speak | spoke |
| spend | spent |
| stand | stood |
| shake | shook |
| swim | swam |
| take | took |
| teach | taught |
| tear | tore |
| tell | told |
| think | thought |
| throw | threw |
| understand | understood |
| wake | woke |
| wear | wore |
| win | won |
| write | wrote |

# Appendix B: The 12 Grammar Tenses in English

| Tense | Example | Form |
|---|---|---|
| Present Simple | My sister *lives* in England.<br>I *am* from Australia. | S + verb(s) + complement<br>S + is/am/are + complement |
| Present Continuous | My sister *is living* in England. | S + is/am/are + verb +ing |
| Present Perfect | My sister *has lived* in England. | S + have/has + past participle |
| Present Perfect Continuous | My sister *has been living* in England for two years. | S + have/has + been + verb-ing |
| Past Simple | My sister *lived* in England. | S + verb+ ed /or irregular form |
| Past Continuous | My sister *was living* in England. | S + was/were + verb-ing |
| Past Perfect | My sister *had lived* in England before she moved to China. | S + had + past participle |
| Past Perfect Continuous | My sister *had been living* in England when she met her husband. | S + had + been + verb-ing |
| Future Simple | My sister *is going to live* in England.<br>My sister *will live* in England. | S + be going to + base verb<br>S + will + base verb |
| Future Continuous | My sister *will be living* in England. | S + will + be + verb-ing |
| Future Perfect | My sister *will have lived* in England for ten years when you come. | S + will + have + past participle |
| Future Perfect Continuous | My sister *will have been living* in England for ten years when you come. | S + will + have + been + verb-ing |

# Appendix C: Review of the Grammar Forms

The following is a chart of the grammar forms for the tenses reviewed in this book.

S = Subject

V = Verb

| Tense | Affirmative | Negative | Question |
|---|---|---|---|
| Present Simple | S + V(s)<br><br>*She understands.* | S + don't/doesn't + base V<br><br>*She doesn't understand.* | (Wh) + do/does + S + base V<br><br>*What does she understand?* |
| Present Continuous | S + is/am/are + V-ing<br><br>*She is reading.* | S + is/am/are + not + V-ing<br><br>*She isn't reading.* | (Wh) + is/am/are + S + V-ing<br><br>*What is she reading?* |
| Future Simple | S + be going to + base V<br>*He's going to eat.*<br><br>S + will + base V<br>*He will eat.* | S + be not going to + base V<br>*He isn't going to eat.*<br><br>S + will not + base V<br>*He won't eat* | (Wh) + is/am/are + S + going to + base V<br>*What is he going to eat?*<br>(Wh) + will + S + base V<br>*What will he eat?* |
| Past Simple | S + verb + ed/ or irregular<br><br>*We tried.* | S + didn't + base V<br><br>*We didn't try.* | (Wh) + did + S + base V<br><br>*Did you try?* |

# Conclusion

Thank you for taking the time to read my book and hopefully you completed the exercises as well. I hope you gained something from this book, and I would appreciate any feedback or questions. My email address is: crystal_carothers@yahoo.com. If you found this book at all useful, I would greatly appreciate your review at Amazon.

Crystal Carothers

Printed in Great Britain
by Amazon